Women In Business

Leading the Way

Copyright © 2020 T&S Publishing, LP

All rights reserved. No portion of this book may be reproduced--mechanically, electronically, or by any other means without the expressed written permission of the authors except as provided by the United States of America copyright law.

Published by **T&S Publishing, LP**

ISBN-9798636904007 **T&S Publishing, LP**

The Publisher has strived to be as accurate and complete as possible in the creation of this book.

This book is not intended for use as a source of legal, business, accounting or financial advice. All readers are advised to seek services of competent professionals in legal, business, accounting, and financial fields.

In practical advice books, like anything else in life, there are no guarantees of income made. Readers are cautioned to rely on their own judgment about their individual circumstances and to act accordingly.

While all attempts have been made to verify information provided in this publication, the Publisher assumes no responsibility for errors, omissions, or contrary interpretation of the subject matter herein. Any perceived slights of specific persons, peoples, or organizations are unintentional.

Table of Contents

INTRODUCTION
    Women in Business- Leading the Way 5

SUZANNE O'BRIEN
    Why OUTSOURCING HR Is Beneficial 14

JOAN BROTHERS
    "It's All About The Clients" 26

MARCI KLEIN
    Riding The Wave Of Entrepreneurship.. 43

AMY REISINGER
    You Don't Know What You Don't Know 59

LETICIA LATINO VAN SPLUNTEREN
    Achieving Confidence In A Male Driven Industry 73

KRISTEN BILLINGSLEY
    Resourcefulness Makes Great Leaders 96

MARIANNE ELLIS
    Say Yes, With Confidence! 110

PATTY TAULBEE
    Wisdom In Decision-Making.. 131

BONNI SHEVIN-SANDY
    Capitalizing On Your Talents - Becoming A Creative Entrepreneur... 142

LAUREN SUSTEK
    Building The Dream Team: Is It Really Possible?.................... 156

JULIET AYDIN MALKI
    Achieve Success As A Mompreneur.. 174

PAMELA STAMBAUGH
It Takes A Village 185
JULIE PARMAR
Marketing Your Business While Building Your Brand 207
APRIL M. DAVIS
Professional Female In A Man's Idustry 224
ACKNOWLEDGMENTS 242

INTRODUCTION

Women in Business- Leading the Way

Women in business continue to change the face of the North American economy. Women are starting more businesses than men and are twice as likely to remain in business as their male counterparts. Career women are thriving and are making a positive impact on the economy. We now represent 55% of university graduates, and 58% of new entrepreneurs.

Advantages Of Women In Business

1. A diverse workforce is an innovative workforce

Diversity—from gender diversity to culture, age, and race—has been shown to foster creativity and innovation. From PricewaterhouseCooper to Disney and L'Oreal, organizations across industries are seeking to prioritize and benefit from a diverse and inclusive work environment.

Men and women will inevitably have different experiences and backgrounds, which shape their approach to business. Challenging each other and collaborating with people who think differently can breed creativity and promote the innovative ideas that push organizations forward.

2. Women excel at the soft skills needed for business leadership

While technical skills and knowledge are fundamental to career success, CEOs consistently cite soft skills as the most desirable professional attributes. Although characteristics like effective communication, empathy, and self-awareness are difficult to measure, they are highly valued and can make a real difference to the bottom line. Recent research has drawn a connection between the strength of character and business performance—with CEOs who rank highly for attributes like compassion and integrity also enjoying a 9.35% return on assets over a two-year period.

Soft skills and emotional intelligence may prove a key competitive advantage for women in business. A 2016 study published by the global consulting firm, Hay Group, found that women outperform men in 11 of 12 key emotional intelligence competencies. These competencies included emotional self-awareness, empathy, conflict management, adaptability, and teamwork—all essential skills for effective leadership in the workplace

3. Women represent huge economic power and offer important consumer insight

It's been estimated that women contribute in excess of $20 trillion in consumer spending every year, representing a bigger growth market than China and India combined. Women also account for 85% of consumer purchases.

Despite this, only 11% of creative directors in advertising are women—up from just 3% in 2008. When Boston Consulting Group did a comprehensive study of the "female economy," it's unsurprising that they found women feel undervalued and underserved by the marketplace. With the power of the female consumer in mind, it's evident that women are best placed to tap into that opportunity and bring valuable consumer insight to the table.

Tapping into the insight both men and women offer can make products and services more marketable and business more profitable. In fact, recent research from McKinsey shows that gender-diverse businesses are 15% more likely to outperform financially above the industry median.

Challenges For Women In Business

1. Women are still underrepresented in key fields

While a number of industries are showing trends of a growing female workforce, sectors like finance, engineering, and tech still tend to be strongly male-dominated. In STEM (science, technology, engineering, and math) industries overall, women make up just 24% of the workforce in the U.S. and less than 15% in the U.K.

2. Gender bias in the workplace

While most executives agree that the best person—regardless of gender—should get the job, the stories of women finding more success with a male or gender-neutral name on their CV demonstrates that unconscious bias still exists.

The women who are in or want to position themselves for leadership roles often feel they come under particular scrutiny. Where men may be encouraged to be ambitious or assertive, women are programmed from a young age not to be "bossy." Underlying gender bias means the same behavior and characteristics—initiative, passion, and taking charge—can be interpreted differently in men and women in the workplace.

Opportunities For Women In Business

We want to help create a world in which every woman and girl can create the kind of life she wishes to lead, unconstrained by harmful norms and stereotypes. We believe a world where women are economically empowered will be a fairer, happier and more prosperous place to live for everybody – and that our business economy will flourish in it.

1. Empowering women can transform the world

Empowering women will transform individual lives, societies – and our businesses. It's essential to the United Nations 2030 Sustainable Development Agenda and its Sustainable Development Goals (SDGs).

Empowering women and girls is the focus of SDG 5, Achieving Gender Equality. But, like the need to work in partnership (SDG 17), women's empowerment is a thread that stitches all the SDGs together.

Our business, too, will be transformed by empowering women. Women are over 70% of our consumer base, 50% of the talent pool from whom we recruit our workforce, and play critical roles in our supply chain and in enabling us to reach consumers with our products. By creating and supporting opportunities for women in society and the economy, we have the possibility to grow our markets, brands, and business.

Gender equality and inclusivity becoming policy

For many forward-thinking organizations, gender equality is becoming a matter of policy, whether it's committing to equal representation of women in the boardroom or hiring diversity officers.

Discouraging and circumventing bias through hiring policy can help organizations to reap the benefits of balance and equality. Rather than political correctness or buzzwords, if diversity, inclusiveness, and gender equality become policy and are embedded in business strategy, businesses thrive.

Making a commitment to things like equitable gender representation, inclusive company culture, and work-life balance—including maternity and paternity benefits—also help organizations to attract top talent. These are a few reasons why companies like Salesforce, General Electric, and Deloitte are cited as excellent places for both women and men to work.

2. Entrepreneurship is the path to leadership

For a growing number of women, the fastest route to the c-suite is launching their own business. In the United States, the number of women-owned businesses has increased 74% over the past 20 years—1.5 times the national average. Today's start-up culture empowers women to be their own boss and pay their own salary, defining how they want to work and making the balance of career and family life easier. Entrepreneurship presents a path for women to close the pay gap and rise to leadership positions, on their own terms.

Running their own company also offers the opportunity for women to collaborate with and hire other ambitious, like-minded women, fostering a new generation of women in leadership roles.

3. Strengthening credentials with a business degree

To stand out in a competitive job market, many women hone the knowledge and expertise they need through a business degree. The number of women enrolling in business school is steadily on the rise. Whether it's undergraduate study, an MBA, EMBA, or master's degree, the business school offers a valuable platform for women to become subject-matter experts, practice leadership skills, and gain the confidence they need to step into the boardroom.

Business school is also an invaluable networking opportunity and a chance to meet mentors in fellow students, professors, and campus speakers. A mentor can offer industry advice and serve as a sounding board for new ideas. Mentors can also become important career sponsors, offering professional opportunities and helping ambitious and talented women to take their next step up the career ladder.

Women Leading the Way in Business

When we think of powerful, influential, positive role model women in our lives, we often think of our mothers, grandmothers, aunts, and teachers. They feed us, nurture us, teach us, and lead us, among many things. When a woman in a developing country is able to generate income or have more control of household spending, she is likely to support her family, through education and healthcare for her children, as well as her community, making an impact beyond just herself.

When a woman runs a business, the same effect can be seen. Many of the characteristics of these positive role model women blend into the way women do business and lead organizations. While women-owned businesses and women-led organizations in the U.S. are still in the minority, the relational impact of their leadership is growing. It's all about connections for many women business owners.

Despite enormous gains made in the past decades, women continue to be woefully underrepresented in positions of power. This is a loss for everyone—important priorities are overlooked and organizations miss out on the range of talent and fresh insights that women can offer.

Women's entrepreneurship will increasingly matter for both business and development. While women still face obstacles to establishing and growing their businesses, the good news is that there now are a variety of documented successful approaches to promoting women's access to finance, training and markets.

Mistakes Women Make In Business

Mistakes can be costly and permanently damage your reputation in the business arena. They are an inevitable part of life and business, but with experience, you can avoid them. The longer you do business, hopefully, the fewer mistakes you will make. The following are seven of the worst mistakes women can make in business and how you can avoid them.

1. Buying into Your Socialization

Women are socialized differently than men, and this reflects in the workplace. Businesswomen must go beyond this cultural socialization to attain their full potential. The "nice girl" attitude you may have learned growing up doesn't work in business, and customers and clients may have a tendency to doubt your abilities or, worse yet, try to take advantage of you. It's important to identify and be clear about your business goals to successfully achieve what you want. You need to focus on and play the specific business game you are engaged in, understand the rules, and then keep it fresh by playing at the edge of the bounds. That's where most games are won.

2. Lacking Confidence

Show a lack of confidence in yourself and your abilities and you may be passed up for profitable opportunities. Women who minimize their accomplishments, constantly apologize, and remain silent in meetings or presentations are going to fail. A lack of confidence, even if you are competent, is like a time bomb and will eventually sabotage your business career.

It's essential to believe in your abilities and have confidence that you can succeed in business. One way to help you get there is to use affirmations several times each day (for at least 21 days) to overcome self-defeating behaviors and habits. Don't expect someone else to tell you that you can do it. Instead, follow your passion in business for your greatest success. Reach out to associates through networking and find a mentor to help build your business strengths. When you don't know the answer to an important question, admit it and say "I will find out the answer and get right back to you."

3. Having a Poor Professional Image

A poor professional image can ruin a woman's business reputation. Your professional image is your identity in the business world. Colleagues, customers, and clients often decide whether to work with you based on their first image or impression of you. Because of this, first impressions can give you a competitive edge or cut you out of the game.

The people you work with like to have a personal sense of who you are. Verbal as well as nonverbal communication, such as posture, greeting, voice tone, gestures, handshake, attitude, and eye contact, comes together to form your professional image. When you are speaking to a group, move slowly and purposefully around the room. Smile and look directly at customers and associates as you speak. Project your voice in a pleasing yet commanding tone, and share anecdotes.

An easy way to polish your professional image is to practice your greetings or presentations in front of a mirror or a video camera. You can see what mistakes you are making and what you are doing right. Also, it creates a professional, cohesive online identity. A website is a good place to build and showcase your abilities. Use networking groups such as LinkedIn and Facebook to list your credentials, education, skills, achievements, and interests. Google yourself and find out what the net is saying about you.

4. Trusting Customers to Pay Their Bills

Trusting people to pay their bills can be a huge mistake. Be sure you know with whom you are doing business. Check them out, and get their D&B credit rating. Never let your customers get too far behind on their payments, even if you are certain they can pay later. When you do suffer a business loss, sometimes it's best to walk away instead of spending a lot of money on lawyers, just to be told you don't have the resources to win the case. Women need to recognize their limitations and options and make the best possible choices.

5. Displaying Negative Emotions

Displaying anger, being rude or egotistical, whining, complaining, and crying will lose you customers. Don't cuss in person, on the phone, or in correspondence, even if your colleagues do. Chances are you will eventually be labeled foul-mouthed. Yelling at or arguing with your customers and associates will label you a hothead or a problem, and you will alienate them. If you only think about yourself or are openly rude, people will run, not walk, in the other direction, and you will pay a heavy price.

Complaining or nagging in business works about as well as it does at home. Women can deal with every challenge in business without complaining, criticizing, yelling, cussing, or being negative. One rule of thumb is to suggest a viable solution instead of criticizing others. Motivate and persuade instead of yelling or bullying to get your point across. Remember to take a couple of deep breaths when you begin to feel overwhelmed; and before you lash out, ask yourself "Is it worth the liability?"

6. Failing to Delegate

Profit most often comes from getting the job done. You don't necessarily have to do the job yourself, but you have to work smart and delegate. Some women are not only afraid to delegate, they just don't know how to ask other people for help. To make matters worse, they also do the work of others. One word of advice: stop.

You need to delegate or you will never expand your business. Identify who can do the job the best for you. Ask, don't tell, people to do something. Be firm and develop a cooperative working effort. In this way, you not only better manage your work, but you also empower the people who work for you so they can excel.

7. Not Investing in Yourself

Not investing in yourself is counterproductive. If you are serious about your value, you will commit a certain amount of money and time to invest in your future. If you don't, you will never find out what you are truly capable of achieving. Pay yourself a good wage and a few well-earned bonuses, and carry adequate insurance to protect you and your business.

Take action steps to ensure your business success. This involves being aware of trends and keeping your eyes and ears open. Look for creative and innovative approaches to solving business problems and taking advantage of opportunities. Women need to step out of their comfort zones and do some research. Develop a plan for investing in yourself and your business, including advertising, consultant fees, new equipment, staff development, and a better business location. Remember to diversify your assets and tap into professional pools by asking your accountant, banker, and lawyer a lot of pertinent questions.

Why OUTSOURCING HR is Beneficial

With SUZANNE O'BRIEN, *CEO OF BLAKE RIAN CONSULTING*

Most business owners agree that their employees are their most valuable assets. As such, managing human resources has become a critical role in managing a business. Yet, for some businesses, the various functions of the HR department are too comprehensive, too costly, and too complex to maintain in-house.

Keep in mind, there are several HR specialty areas, including payroll, recruiting, benefits, compliance, and more. In some businesses, an HR generalist may be asked to perform more than one of these HR functions, and that can often result in less than optimal results.

Human resources management is an important, but complex, function for any company, and one that many opt to outsource. Although outsourcing HR might not be right for all businesses, there are some significant advantages to doing so, especially when it comes to saving time and money.

Most companies that outsource human resources functions do so by joining a Staffing company who handles everything from hiring and onboarding employees to managing benefits, developing training programs and overseeing compliance with employment rules and regulations.

The benefits of outsourcing HR are plentiful and can have a significant impact on your bottom line.

How the Internet has helped with Outsourcing

Suzanne recalls conversations with people where she says, "I remember when the Internet first surfaced and we thought oh my gosh, what a crazy fad that will never last! LOL!" Now we see every person using a mobile device, laptop, or tablet and connecting with the whole world in real real-time with the help of the Internet. Without any doubt, the Internet was the single biggest invention by a human in history, period. It changed the course of our lives, our businesses, and every other thing that has an impact on our life one way or another.

People no longer are going door to door seeking a job. Help Wanted signs outside your business are obsolete. Even though the Internet has made job searching a bit easier, it has not made the challenge of filling the right person into the right job any less of a challenge nor any less time time-consuming. And as a business leader, who has the time and resources nowadays to fill vacancies within their company?

Outsourcing

Outsourcing -- the practice of using outside firms to handle work commonly performed within a company -- is a familiar concept to many entrepreneurs. Small companies routinely outsource their payroll processing, accounting, distribution, and many other important functions -- often because they have no other choice. Many large companies turn to outsource to cut costs. In response, entire industries have evolved to serve companies' outsourcing needs. Employers also spend an enormous amount of money and time on hiring—an average of $4,129 and 52 days to hire per job in the United States, according to Society for Human Resource Management estimates, and many times that amount for managerial roles—and the United States fills a staggering 66 million jobs a year.

Not many businesses thoroughly understand the benefits of outsourcing. Outsourcing can indeed save money, but that's not the only (or even the most important) reason to do it.

Here are some of the advantages you'll receive from outsourcing with Blake Rian Consulting.

Focus can remain on your business

Taking time out to focus on recruiting new employees can result in neglecting your usual job, which could be important to the running of the company. It can cost companies thousands of dollars if employees are taking on the responsibility of their role and additional roles. . This results in a drop in productivity and a deficiency in morale as their own work gets pushed to the side. By outsourcing your recruitment, you can leave the job to the recruiter to fill openings quicker. This eliminates other people from having to cover and allows you to attend to your usual business.

Improve the Quality Candidates

The most important reason to partner with a staffing company like Blake Rian Consulting is to get access to better talent. Staffing agencies have the means and resources required to locate top performers. Top Performers who can help you on your road to success and the skills needed to choose the right candidates. Not only for the open positions you have but also for your company as a whole. When you outsource staffing services, you get to benefit from the hiring expertise and experience of recruiters.

Level the playing field.

Most small firms simply can't afford to match the in-house support services that larger companies maintain. Outsourcing can help small firms act "big" by giving them access to the same economies of scale, efficiency, and expertise that large companies enjoy.

Reduce turnover rate

A poorly run recruitment process could be to blame for a high turnover rate, which can have financial implications for a business, as well as disruptions to productivity and ongoing projects. A high turnover may not necessarily be a reflection on your company in general, as it may just indicate that candidates just aren't a perfect fit for the company or that management is not nurturing them as they should!

Recruiters are well-practiced in assessing what kind of people will be suitable for a particular role and the company culture, so it could assist in placing individuals who are better suited to the business and will stay in the job for longer

Faster Hiring and Keeping up with Demand

Having positions left open for a long time can hurt your bottom line. Reduced productivity can not only lead to lost opportunities, but it can also reduce your current workforce's morale and efficiency. When your employees have to take on a bigger workload and work longer hours while you continue to search for new hires, they can become irritable, stressed, and unhappy. Their own productivity will suffer. And they might even think about leaving your company.

When you outsource staffing services, you won't have to deal with these consequences. You'll get faster hiring because staffing firms already have extensive candidate pools and top talent to call on. They'll start working immediately to find you a new employee. They won't get distracted with other responsibilities and tasks like your managers or HR specialists would. They'll be fully dedicated to the hiring process, without delay, and without procrastination, so you can fill those positions more quickly.

Lower Costs

Outsourcing your staffing services won't be free, but the cost you'll pay will be significantly less than all of the costs associated with hiring and training new employees in-house. All of the costs of recruiting, advertising, interviewing, background checking, and skills testing will be rolled into one easy-to-manage fee.

Also, outsourcing your hiring to the experts can reduce your costs of training as the candidates they find will have the skills and experience needed to get the job done right from the very start. Since recruiters consider factors and qualities that ensure long-term hires, you'll also reduce your costs of turnover. Finally, because the staffing firm will take care of compliance, payroll, and HR for its workers, you will also save on administrative and overhead costs. It pays to outsource.

Workforce Flexibility

You might have a mountain of work one week, but no work at all the following week. One of the benefits of outsourcing staffing services is that it's easier than ever to get temporary workers when you need them. When you hire temp workers, you can fulfill your current needs, but without the financial commitment of continuous employment. You can increase or decrease your workforce whenever your workload calls for it.

Temp-to-Perm Opportunities

Any time you've made a hiring mistake and onboarded the wrong candidate it tends to be a very costly mistake. That cost can fall under many different areas; time, money and productivity. . You've probably thought to yourself how great it would be to be able to test out your new hires for a few weeks before extending an offer of employment. When you partner with a staffing firm, you can take advantage of temp-to-perm opportunities. You can bring on new workers, test them out in your workplace, and then make the decision to hire them on permanently or not. This can significantly reduce your risks of bad hiring decisions and the consequences that come with these risks.

Reduce risk.

Every business investment carries a certain amount of risk. Markets, competition, government regulations, financial conditions, and technologies all change very quickly. Outsourcing providers assume and manage this risk for you, and they generally are much better at deciding how to avoid risk in their areas of expertise.

Who is Blake Rian Consulting:

Blake Rian Consulting is a mediator firm between a jobseeker and employer from the State of Washington. Blake Rian Consulting is neither new nor a small name in this field. The Firm's CEO, Suzanne O' Brien, has been associated with the industry for over 13 years.

Suzanne O'Brien (CEO) has managed some large corporations. Suzanne has also focused on expanding her knowledge through extensive training, seminars, and masterclasses to use the acquired knowledge to grow her Businesses.

Blake Rian Consulting offers unparalleled hiring services to place the right people with the right companies. They provide an efficient, effective, and enjoyable experience to job seekers and their employers. They have never deferred from their motto:

"We firmly believe it is not about putting someone in the seat. It is about finding the right fit."

The basic purpose and goal of Blake Rian Consulting is to understand the needs of the employers and job seekers to help bring together the perfect match in expertise, skill, and company culture fit. "We know that a resume is important, but it's also just a blueprint of someone's experience."

It was found that one of the biggest challenges that Blake Rian Consulting heardfrom their clients is that recruiters do not understand our business.

Blake Rian Consulting consists of subject matter experts, and its process is transparent and easy to understand. Blake Rian Consulting learns and understands your business and what success looks like in your next hire. Blake Rian Consulting partners with its clients to ensure finding the right fit.

Currently, Blake Rian Consulting is based and headquartered in Bellevue, Washington State. The Company currently employs about 50 people in Bellevue, Washington, and it has created a business for hundreds of clients in Washington. Since launching Blake Rian Consulting, they have received such enormous positive feedback from their clients, either the employer or the employee, that they have decided to expand and extend their services to other parts of the United States.

Suzanne O'Brien, Founder/CEO of Blake Rian Consulting, has decided to expand and open a brand-new office in the City of Newport Beach in the Sunshine State of California. With such a proven track record in Staffing services, they have everything that's required to conquer the market in Newport Beach. With veterans like Suzanne, it would be an excellent venture for the Company, its future, and its reputation.

Who is SUZANNE O'BRIEN?

Suzanne O'Brien has been in the Human Resource industry for over 13 years. She has managed some large corporations during her tenure. Suzanne's job is to understand the needs of the employers and job seekers to help bring together the perfect match of expertise, skill, and company culture fit. Her primary goal is to help her target audience break the barriers and fears of starting their businesses and having it all with the motive of showing everyone that you can use technology and adapt to the changing business market without sacrificing long term client partnerships. Blake Rian Consulting provides an efficient, effective, and enjoyable experience to jobseekers and employers. It is known as a Women-owned Company partnering with clients in all industries nationwide.

Conversation with Suzanne O'Brien, *CEO of Blake Rian Consulting*

Suzanne, running a successful staffing agency has its challenges, can you share with us your ideal client

Suzanne: My Client base has four divisions right now. We have the Professional Services division, where we focus on HR, Finance, Marketing, and Customer Service position in a contract and direct hire capacity.

The second division is our Hospitality division. Here we focus on Corporate Catering and Event Services.

The third division is our Payroll division. Here we take on the administrative side of people working for clients. If they have interns or perhaps, they want to bring someone they know or a previous worker back for a project. We handle the payroll and all administrative tasks that accompany bringing that person on board.

Managed Services is our fourth division. A Managed Service is a contingent worker program (temporary staffing) of a client company by managing its preferred staffing projects. It can consist of a team of program managers and coordinators that help the client company source and manage temporary workers. Contingent or On-Demand talent, as you so often hear employees referred to, can help you fix important voids in personnel, support company goals, and initiatives, and drive productivity. One of the Managed Services we provide is a Recruiter. We have a dedicated Recruiter who fills your internal roles and essentially works as your internal employee. This allows you to fill positions quickly and uniformly under your company vs. paying an hourly bill rate for a Contract Recruiter or a Direct Fee per position. Blake Rian Consulting helps clients understand when they move towards a Managed Service; their projects are more resourceful, cost and time efficient, and productive.

Success comes in all forms; what does success look like to you?

Suzanne: Success, to me, is building long-lasting partnerships. It is helping clients and the right talent to help build their business. It is helping someone find that perfect job that gives them the means to take care of their family. My goal with Blake Rian is to build something I am passionate about and pass it along to my children. Helping people along the way is really what I love about this industry and this business.

Any industry has its own challenges or obstacles. What is an issue with your industry, and how is Blake Rian Consulting overcoming that issue?

Suzanne: I think a big problem within my industry is everything has become so transactional. It has become a numbers game with talent and clients. Staffing has become a bad word. There is the connotation that Staffing companies overcharge and/or inflate their bill rates or fees and don't care about making a good fit. Unfortunately, in some cases, that is true. I understand at the end of the day, businesses are for-profit, and you must make money. I think there is a way to have the best of both worlds. Instead of being the biggest, why not be the best?

Blake Rian Consulting is overcoming this issue in the way we approach our clients and candidates. We strive to partner with both sides and get an idea of what is truly important to the client and the candidate. That is really where I came up with my tag line.

We firmly believe it is not about putting someone in the seat. It is about finding the right fit.

With a lot of corporations, it comes down to how much margin we can make. I have seen it cost clients great candidates and companies, great clients. Blake Rian Consulting is the company you partner with long term and refer to your friends, not the company that you used once and had an okay experience with a high price tag.

As a successful Business Leader in your own industry, what advice do you have for someone who is looking at going into Entrepreneurship?

Suzanne: The best advice I can give is to start a business you are really passionate about and do your due diligence. I wish I would have invested in certain software and back-office items sooner and saved some growing pains.

What advice would you share with a potential client when they are shopping you and your fellow competitors?

Suzanne: I would tell them to review everything we offer and compare it to other companies. Ask the questions around background screenings, interviewing, and do not be afraid to ask about pricing. Any company can do something with a higher price tag, that does not mean it is a better service. I would also say do not be afraid of working with a smaller company. To a smaller company, a customer can be much more valued and taken care of. There is more flexibility around services without jeopardizing quality.

You previously stated you had expanded Blake Rian Consulting to include a Hospitality division where your focus is Corporate Catering and Event Services. Can you what services you provide and why you expanded in that direction?

Suzanne: In our Hospitality division, we focus on Front of House and Back of House roles in a Catering company. Anything from Cooks, Dishwashers to Catering Assistants up to Director level roles. We expanded with Division as we saw a need in the market for this type of business. There are "Hospitality" Staffing companies, and our clients worked with them. What we found is they had a huge issue with reliability, quality of staff, and a revolving door of new peoplecoming in. We were able to remove those pain points and provide them quality candidates, quality candidates, without a considerable cost to their budget. We also work with them on payrolling people that they are interested in bringing on. We found this need in CA as well, and that is why we expanded there first.

Where do you see your business in 3 to 5 years from now?

Suzanne: I am constantly thinking of new and fresh ways to recruit talent. I am also continuously working on my current client partnerships and building new ones. I am focusing one day at a time and pushing forward. However, I see more locations opening with fully functional teams. I also have recently been certified through WBENC, where I get to connect with other Women Business Leaders, and the support and opportunities will help grow Blake Rain Consulting.

What do you feel is your secret key to the success of Blake Rain Consulting?

Suzanne: I am very passionate about what I do and genuinely care about my employees and clients. I am very determined and strive to be the very best at what I do. I started my staffing career at the bottom and worked hard to get to where I am now. I am very grateful every day for the opportunities I have been given. My support system within my family is incredible. My desire is to build a Legacy for my children.

Contact Suzanne O'Brien

Phone: (206) 948-0614
Email: suzanne@blakerianconsulting.com
Website: https://www.blakerianconsulting.com/
LinkedIn: https://pk.linkedin.com/company/blake-rian-consulting

Boutique Is Best
"IT'S ALL ABOUT THE CLIENTS"
JOAN BROTHERS, CEO
MANHATTAN BOUTIQUE REAL ESTATE (MBRE)

These days, businesses are constantly changing. The opportunity is discovering new ways to keep up. In the service economy, it has never been more apparent that, if you want to thrive, you must continuously evolve, listen, and grow to stay in step with your clients. As a service provider, our job seems simple: MBRE's motto summarizes it - **"IT'S ALL ABOUT THE CLIENTS!"**

Joan Brothers, CEO of Manhattan Boutique Real Estate (MBRE), learned early on in her real estate career that clients could make or break you. From finding and converting leads to keeping clients happy and retaining them for future business or referrals, sometimes it feels like an uphill climb. Throughout Joan's experience of launching and running a real estate brokerage firm, she has discovered the secret behind small business success and finding opportunities.

As publisher of the book, I sat down with Joan to discover some insights about MBRE, herself as a businesswoman in New York, and her dealings and relationships with her clients. Here are my takeaways on the topics that we discussed.

How to Evaluate Your Client's Needs?

How can we possibly meet clients' needs intelligently and drive real value if we, the enablers, do not spend the time to learn what matters most to them? What are the problems that a real estate agency needs to solve for their client? How do you create your value in the eyes of that client?

It takes a particular type of leader to expose themselves to a client in a way that most business owners will not. I think of it as being confident in your vulnerability. If anyone thinks this sounds like an oxymoron, they are right. People are more likely to connect with you not only in life but in business if you are willing to talk to them honestly about what drives them. These types of conversations develop trust and relationships. These connections are the brick and mortar of the foundation on which loyalty and collaboration are built.

It is easy to start by asking a client the obvious questions, such as "What is your budget? What kind of property are you seeking? What are your objectives such as main home, office space, investment property?" All of these questions are important, but everyone in your organization should ask these questions. Go to the next level by asking a client more in-depth questions - get to know them! Look for new ways to help them, not just yourself. Constantly re-evaluate services to make them better.

How to Tailor Your Services to Your Client

The client-first model means helping clients figure out how to fulfill their needs. Focus on finding new ways to collaborate and narrow the gap between ideas and execution with the sole purpose of enabling them to create more value - create more, produce more, engage with the customers more, and ultimately sell more.

You also have to ask yourself if you, as a business, can accommodate your clients' needs, not only now but later? What happens when they grow? Can your business grow with them? For business owners, the most important thing is to have an exit plan. It is the opposite of reading a good novel. In business, you want to have a clear picture of the end of the story so you can anticipate the plot twists and manage them effectively.

It is precisely the same with clients. Sit down with them in the beginning and ask them what their exit strategy might be. Tell them that this will help you both plan for a long and prosperous relationship. What happens if, as a result of your partnership, your client finds tremendous success early on? As a business owner, are you committed to growth and expansion in sync with your client? Make a business plan for your organization that shows how you would tailor your services and pipeline to your customers as they grow. Always look for new ways to refresh your service offering, even if it means disrupting the status quo. Listen and adjust. Remind yourself it is all about your clients, period. You won't have a business without them, so keep thinking of new ways to serve their ever-changing needs.

How to have success with a Small Business Perspective

Joan shared this about her company: "We are a boutique agency by choice. We keep our roster small, so we can give our clients the attention they deserve."

Many small companies strive to grow bigger. But companies can be more competitive in serving both small and big clients while maintaining their status of being a boutique. How can a small business retain its culture and values shared throughout the company when it grows in terms of clients and expanding business? Is it possible to keep a small business culture in a large business world?

By maintaining open communication and creating a positive work environment, a business will maintain satisfied and repeat customers.

I discussed with Joan seven steps a business owner can take to ensure their boutique style business continues to thrive no matter the size.

1. Promote Shared Beliefs with Your Team

Small businesses have a culture, unlike midsize and larger companies, usually with a positive, laid-back attitude that encompasses a family-like atmosphere. Although this relaxed environment may be in jeopardy as a company grows, there are ways to maintain this small business feeling in a midsize business environment. Starting from the top, management should create a set of shared beliefs throughout the company, which includes establishing a framework for how to make decisions, set company priorities, and how to treat co-workers.

One way to maintain these shared cultural beliefs is by writing them down and disseminating them. These core values can serve as a constant reminder of the shared beliefs that should be upheld throughout the company. Also, the old saying of "actions speak louder than words" is integral in a company—management needs to lead by example and uphold company-shared cultural beliefs. Quarterly training of these values may be necessary to remind managers how to guide the office culture as it grows. Instilling small business values throughout the management base will help to preserve this small business feeling inside a midsize organization.

2. Make Sure your Team Treats Customers with a Small Business Perspective

Shared company beliefs are not only important within the business walls, but also outside of the company. Small businesses have a reputation for showing empathy, understanding and being responsive to customers. However, as a company grows, that personal touch may be lost when customers are dealing with a different employee for each and every business need. Employees need to be reminded that, although the company is growing, it is critical they see things from a small business perspective and support customers' needs on a personal level.

3. Manage Communication between Your Team and the Clients

Real estate small businesses such as MBRE usually have an open-door policy in which an independent contractor (IC) feels comfortable connecting with the manager to discuss company issues informally and frequently. As the number of people grows within the company, however, this ease of communication can be stifled, and employees (or IC, if that applies to your business) may get compartmentalized into a specific role within the company. Employees may feel replaceable, and that can diminish the loyalty they felt in a small business atmosphere. As companies grow, it is imperative managers maintain an open-door policy to preserve communication and help employees feel they are respected. Encourage them to go to their managers with any questions or concerns. Throughout the day, managers should demonstrate their availability and willingness to discuss issues either through email, memos, or verbally.

When a business grows, it can also be hard to maintain close connections with employees. To avoid this loss of commitment, management should strive to communicate with employees daily. Although midsize and large companies tend to focus on objectives in lieu of their employees, managers and supervisors should be instructed to communicate with employees on a personal level. This can be accomplished by having weekly meetings, whether it is over a coffee break, at lunchtime, via email, over the phone, or a simple visit during the workday. Talking about everything from the weekend to the weather will maintain a familiarity within the company. Keeping an open-door policy will help maintain a small business culture.

4. Involve Your Team

Keeping employees apprised of company decisions will help maintain a small business culture that promotes unity within the company and helps keep employees engaged in the welfare of the business. For example, employees that have a strong understanding of the profit and loss perspectives of the company will have a sense of entitlement within the company, which is good for promoting positive morale. By organizing a specific time and place to convene and allowing employees to contribute ideas and goals, such as by email or during informal weekly meetings, employees will feel as if they are needed within the company. They will avoid feeling either underappreciated or ignored in the business setting. Large companies retain a small company atmosphere by giving their employees a specific purpose and allowing them to contribute ideas and help solve problems.

5. Recognize and Reward Your Team

Giving recognition for a job well done sometimes disappears as a company grows, but it is imperative to continue to recognize employees in front of their peers. This can be done by recognizing an employee of the month in a company newsletter or during a regular staff meeting so that the employee's peers can acknowledge a job well done. In addition, incentives should be provided regularly, such as giving tickets to an event. Employees will feel more appreciated and motivated as the company continues to grow.

6. Support your Local Community – Think Outside of Your Company

When a company grows, it is harder for employees to get to know who they work with on a day-to-day basis. Activities outside of the office can help build camaraderie and introduce employees to their counterparts in a fun, relaxed setting. Whether it is a holiday office party, midsummer barbeque, or impromptu catered lunch, growing the company's culture through events that are not company-related will allow employees to bond on a more personal level. This feeling of being connected can help develop and improve employee morale and promote small business culture in a midsize to a large business setting. By always being part of something bigger than yourself, supporting your local community can tie your company and its team to a more significant cause, which is very rewarding. Joan gave an excerpt of how MBRE supported a local neighborhood.

"We love supporting local causes, especially ones that bring everybody in the neighborhood together, and that is exactly what the *Taste of Sutton* event does. As a local resident and real estate boutique owner, I take great pride in the continued development of the Sutton Place area and community, including the wonderful buildings, restaurants, and retail.

We commend the Sutton Area Community (SAC) on its mission "to actively engage residents and business establishments in efforts to maintain and enhance the quality of life in the community." We were delighted to become members of SAC and even more pleased to be a sponsor of the first-ever *Taste of Sutton*!"

7. Maintain a Small Business Culture

A company's culture and beliefs should maintain a focus that helps employees feel trusted and appreciated, as this will allow the company to maintain quality employees and satisfied customers. Communication throughout the organization is the key to keeping a small business culture within a growing organization and for making employees feel valued through communication, recognition, and incentives. They will stay motivated, productive, and enthusiastic as the company grows.

Who is Joan Brothers?

Joan Brothers, CEO, founded Manhattan Boutique Real Estate (MBRE), which is based in New York City (NYC).

"There is nothing more exciting than connecting fascinating people to spectacular homes and investments in our great city!"

She enjoys the process from the first hello, to the art of negotiation, to handing keys over for each unique property. With a combination of international focus from family, an MBA, corporate experience at Mitsui, and a chance introduction to real estate, she began over 20 years ago focusing her energies and entrepreneurial spirit in the residential real estate business.

Her successes include being voted into "Who's Who in Luxury Real Estate," and for having represented many high-profile entertainers, diplomats, financial and corporate businesspeople, and governments worldwide. MBRE shows how a SMALL company can successfully represent and serve BIG clients.

She helps both American and international clients make their NYC real estate assets work for them. Excelling in luxury condominium rentals and sales, corporate relocations, as well as development and preconstruction sales, she and her clients have access to every new construction property built in NYC.

Her experience also includes brokering commercial office space, retail leasing, building sales, real estate consultation, and raising capital for development. MBRE is active in providing both in equity and debt from institutional investors such as Goldman Sachs and Citibank.

MBRE's combination of their ability to do financial analysis and negotiation, plus Joan's international flair and intercultural understanding, make her a key ally for any client who wants to navigate the complex NYC real estate market.

She is a graduate of Miss Porter's School, has a BA from Boston College, and an MBA from UHBS-Paris, France, and the University of Hartford.

She resides in Manhattan and is an active community member of the Asia Society, Civitas, and The Real Estate Board of NY (REBNY) Small Firms Committee. She has served on the Board of Directors for her apartment building, her child's PTA, and, currently, the East Midtown Neighborhood Coalition. Her hobbies include travel, skiing, and an appreciation of Chinese and various cultures.

With more than 20 years of service in NYC's real estate industry, MBRE was selected as the winner in the Real Estate Agency category of Best of Manhattan Awards for 2019.

What is Manhattan Boutique Real Estate (MBRE)?

"We are a boutique agency by choice. We keep our roster small, so we can give our clients the attention they deserve."

MBRE is a full-service firm that offers a transparent, intimate approach to buying, selling, and renting properties in NYC. They understand the needs of their clients, both global and local, and are ready to guide buyers, sellers, landlords, and renters through this market. MBRE has experts in residential, commercial, consulting, and real estate development. They also focus on Real Estate Advisory Services. MBRE is a certified Women Business Enterprise (WBE) and approved as *"Best for NYC."*

- **Local Expertise and Networks with Global Knowledge.**

MBRE differentiates themselves in the NYC condominium, cooperative, and townhouse markets by how they work with investors, buyers, sellers, renters, and landlords. Utilizing their global knowledge and real estate expertise, MBRE personalizes service to each client's specific needs. They have represented individuals, countries, and corporations from over 20 states within the U.S. and over 30 countries. The MBRE team has a combined total of more than 75 years of experience and has completed over $200 million in various types of real estate transactions.

- **We Go Beyond the Deal.**

The NYC real estate market is unique. MBRE clients rely on the team to address fundamental as well as more complex needs, such as how to maximize the value of their NYC real estate. MBRE has a value-added network which includes connecting to accountants, attorneys, bankers, contractors, architects, school consultants, and more.

- **We Lead to Success.**

With an eye on global news and local trends combined with market expertise, MBRE educates its clients on what makes NYC neighborhoods and properties unique.

- **We Value Long Term Relationships.**

The MBRE team takes great pride in guiding clients through a smooth "process" to realize their real estate vision. The business-client relationship continues long after the deal is done.

Q & A: A Conversation with JOAN BROTHERS CEO of Manhattan Boutique Real Estate (MBRE)

Would you share some insight into your love for New York City?

Joan: One of my favorite quotes is, *"I would give the greatest sunset in the world for one sight of New York's skyline. The sky over New York and the will of man-made visible."* Ayn Rand

I find NYC so energizing and exciting - the streets, the people, the activities, and the options of how you can enjoy life and conduct business. I wake up every morning, and it is an "anything can happen day!"

Who or what inspired you to start MBRE?

Joan: I remember a very good friend who said, "You have nothing to lose!" She meant it in the nicest of ways, and I felt so liberated that if there were a failure, it would be ok. It made that first step seem simple.

My father was always supportive of me, and I appreciated that he encouraged me each step of the way from when I was a young girl to the present. He would make it seem so special, "You're the first person in our family to... So now think about your next step to..." Having that support and taking things step-by-step made it seem manageable.

My personal life also dictated finding the best options for me. Having a child helped inspire me to start my own company. I was still working as hard as ever for someone else, but I could see that certain things were going to have to change for me to enjoy a work/life balance. The change came when my aunt offered to take care of my son, and I was able to build my own company on my own terms confidently.

With an expansion mindset, I have ventured into new businesses relating to real estate. In 2017, MBRE was picked and listed as one of the MWBE companies allowed to help with affordable housing utilizing NYC HPD city land. In 2018, I saw an opportunity to get involved in introducing artists from China into spaces in NYC art galleries. In 2019, we created Smart NY Solutions, a technology and marketing company that helps cities and businesses connect the community through the Internet of Things (IoT), digital signage, wayfinding, and content.

What are the biggest barriers you have faced with MBRE? Also, tell us about an obstacle you faced while growing your business?

Joan: The biggest challenge to my business is finding agents to work in the company that represents the high value we place on customer service. I need to trust them to work with the clients in the same way that I would. Hands down, that is the most challenging obstacle for me. It is not uncommon for us to work with many generations within a family. We are genuinely long-term advisors with our clientele!

The real estate brokerage business is continuously changing because of local and national government policy. A recent example of a change in policy is the state and local tax (SALT) deduction, which allows taxpayers to deduct local tax payments on their federal tax returns. The new tax plan called the Tax Cuts and Jobs Act instituted a cap on the SALT deduction. Starting with the 2018 tax year, the maximum SALT deduction available was $10,000. Previously, there was no limit, so this has affected homeowners in high-tax states such as New York. Buyers now consider this factor and it affects selling prices.

Additionally, the cost of advertising is high though it has changed in recent years. Also, you need to have a dedicated person to utilize social media to engage clients. We employ an outside firm that stays on top of the latest trends to guide us, so our marketing dollars work the best.

Another challenge is performing day-to-day functions. As our business grows, so does the "to do" list. I am so appreciative that I have a team that helps manage the many business requirements, social media, and the chaos that can come on any given day. It requires finding trustworthy people who can handle daily challenges beyond real estate (for example, government registration and general business details) so the focus can remain on the client.

How is the disruption economy affecting real estate?

Joan: You cannot continue with the old ways if they are stale and no longer work, so you always have to reinvent yourself and your way of doing business.
Arthur Miller's play *Death of a Salesman* rings true. "The only thing you've got in this world is what you can sell," Charley told Willy Loman.

Real estate is constantly inundated with players attempting to disrupt the business. However, buying and renting real estate properties is very different in NYC than elsewhere. The perils of a misstep are so high that it requires a trusted guide.

MBRE is valuable to our busy and successful clients because they do not have a great deal of time and need to task someone with the job of finding them a home while having a fiduciary responsibility to them.

Understandably, people want to find ways to save money, and business models that seek to help people with this are desirable. What impresses me about the Millennial, which is the newest group of consumers, is that they seek out a "consultant." In this case, a real estate expert helps them go through the process from start to finish. They most definitely start online and view properties they like, but they share them with their trusted advisor who helps them secure the property. Realtor.com says 90% of home buyers searched online during their home buying process.

It is also understandable why disrupters try to penetrate the real estate market. To gain a better perspective on what kind of money is behind Proptech, in 2019, real estate tech start-ups raised $3.4 billion in funding (up 5x from 2013 per CB Insights).

As an example, Zillow, which owns the NYC local listing site Streeteasy, seeks to have direct communications with clients. In my opinion, their goal is to control the client so, as the disrupter, they can connect the client to the "right" person. What that translates into is an agent or company must pay Zillow (or any like company) for the connection. Zillow makes money and serves its own interest by stopping the direct flow of a buyer connecting to the property's broker. The client is not necessarily taken care of, and their best interests may or may not be served. This is not an optimum system for the buyer, renter agent, or broker, but this is how control from a tech company works. So, the goal to "cut out the middleman" has been supplanted with a tech company inserting itself into the middle to extract a fee from one side (the broker) in numerous ways without giving a definite benefit to the consumer. In my opinion, the models of disrupters continually change, but the results are the same for the end-user.

There are low-fee commission brokerage firms that have started up businesses in other cities. They have not gotten much traction in NYC due to the unique complications of coops and condo rules, which require much more work and know-how.

Various studies are stating how artificial intelligence can replace all sorts of jobs. With the current status quo, I am sure that real estate agents are in jeopardy, too.

MBRE is consistently utilizing new technologies that help us efficiently and effectively communicate and provide service to our valued clients. An example would be a new app called Realty Crunch, which organizes and allows you and your client to communicate directly about specific properties. It is like Trello but for real estate.

It is all about "staying on your toes!"

What sets MBRE apart from the other real estate agencies?

Joan: In NYC, there is no shortage of competition in terms of the actual number of people in the real estate brokerage business. I created Manhattan Boutique Real Estate (MBRE) to make sure that people understood our motto, **"We are all about our clients."** In the service business, you need to represent your clients. You need to understand their specific needs and where they are heading in their career and personal life, so you can guide them to make the right decisions in the short and long-term. This is always how you stand out; make sure your clients are a few steps ahead of where they need to be.

I've enjoyed being a trusted advisor to clients at different stages of their life. It is incredibly fulfilling to be with them each step of the way for their personal and professional growth and be of service in each transaction.

Sometimes it is not about a person but a country. I have represented several Missions to the United Nations. I have met world leaders from Ambassadors to the Head of the General Assembly to various royal family members. This is a profoundly personal and private relationship where you need to look at their individual needs and position. I feel that securing the diplomats an appropriate residence allows them to focus on their job, which is very important as they strive for world peace!

In addition, we have helped world renown Art Galleries to Fortune 500 Corporations to Family Foundations develop their strategies for their real estate needs for purchasing and renting.

While being successful does mean earning a commission, it is also gaining the client's trust and a long-term relationship, which many times culminate in a lasting friendship.

What advice would you provide to potential Entrepreneurs that want to break into the real estate industry?

Joan: Keep an eye open for opportunities in an area where you can add value. I would suggest finding a mentor in a growing segment of the market and neighborhood, building your network, becoming an expert in your product, and knowing your clients. Understand that it is not about just about earning money; it is about helping families, businesses, and your community. With this in mind, you will always have a continuous stream of happy clients.

What advice do you have for potential clients when they are looking for a firm to handle their real estate needs?

Joan: Our clients tell us they appreciate our understanding of their unique situations and coming up with opportunities for them.

We have an extended team that can handle their specific needs.

We are your local expert for NYC real estate. We are a full-service firm that offers a clear, intimate approach to buying, selling, and renting properties in NYC. We understand the needs of our global and local clients and are ready to guide buyers, sellers, landlords, and renters throughout this market. We have experts in residential, commercial, consulting, and real estate development. We also focus on Real Estate Advisory Services.

Interacting with a diverse client base, with an eye on global news and local trends combined with market expertise, we educate our clients on what makes NYC neighborhoods and properties special and unique.

What is the next step for you?

Joan: Interacting with my clientele in the realm of real estate gives me great joy. I would never give that up. As an entrepreneur, I believe in always keeping your eyes open for opportunities and expanding on what you have built.

One problem I saw was that luxury housing was plentiful, but the middle or lower-priced housing was lacking in NYC and also how the local communities need support.

I began to see the problem when I started working with my clients' adult children. My clients lived in luxury Manhattan condos, but when it came to their children, they only wanted Brooklyn, which was perceived as a much hipper location. In exploring these areas, I understood how each community was essential to each neighborhood. As affluence moved into more popular but middle-class locations, it was also important to preserve the existing neighborhood culturally.

MBRE was able to get approved from NYC as a woman-owned company, which was one of 29 companies listed and allowed to work with city land for affordable workforce housing since 2017.

Also, understanding changing workforce needs and the need for Community + Technology + Real Estate prompted the formation of Smart

NY Solutions Inc., a joint-venture, women-owned business MWBE, which we define as Smart City Consultants.

Smart NY enhances communications using digital solutions. The clients are cities and businesses that want to enhance communication, navigation, accessibility, and create a viable economic workforce. We use experiential technology (such as AI and IoT) to develop smart city or business spaces to improve the quality of life for people living, working, and visiting.

Contact Joan Brothers

Phone Number: (212) 308-2482
Cell Number: (917) 517-2316
Email: jb@mbreny.com
Website URL: https://mbreny.com/
Facebook Link: https://www.facebook.com/manhattanbre
Twitter Link: https://twitter.com/MBRErealestate
LinkedIn: https://www.linkedin.com/company/manhattan-boutique-real-estate/
Instagram: mbreny
Skype: Joanbrothers
WhatsApp: Joan Brothers
WeChat: Joan Brothers

RIDING THE WAVE OF ENTREPRENEURSHIP

With MARCI KLEIN, CEO OF KLEIN CREATIVE MEDIA

Not everyone dreams of being an entrepreneur. For Marci Klein, owning her own business was not her aspiration in the beginning. But just like the currents of the ocean, she was swept away on a journey she hadn't anticipated.

The Beginning-Discovering Her Passion

When Marci started surfing, she never knew what a transformative life experience it would be for her. She has done a lot of sports, i.e., competitive tennis, volleyball, snowboarding, scuba diving, yet none even compare to surfing.

"Sunrise is the best time to start my weekly adventures. Although early mornings it's tough to brace for the shocking cold...it's almost always worth it...surfing is like pizza, even when it's bad, it's good.

It was over three decades ago that I both discovered my life passion for surfing and declared myself a video production major at UC San Diego. I remember climbing down the rocky trail to Black's Beach with a foam surfboard under my arm. I can still feel the warm fall sunshine and the smell of the beach as I paddled into the ocean as a beginner surfer. I had butterflies in my stomach because even though I love the beach, I never lost the fear of the waves, having been held under as a child. But I go for it anyway. Because that's who I am. Paddling into the whitewash, I pop up to my feet immediately, like I was borne to ride, just like I still do today. The feeling of catching a wave is euphoric. Your exhilarated, your heart is pumping, yet it's peaceful just past the breakers, unlike any peace on land. And it's beautiful. Over 30 years later, being on the beach still gives me the same high, the same Zen, a feeling that I belong in the water.

When I graduated college to begin my TV career, producing and directing reality TV, I tried to live inland to be close to Hollywood. Still, I felt the draw of the ocean, and it led me to the South Bay, where I now call home to both my family and my video production studio.

I find inspiration for my client's stories from the ocean - in it or soaring above it in a light sport trike, or with my drone. The ocean gives me energy, freckles, and keeps me young at heart. It is where most of my scripts are written in my head, long before my hands ever reach a computer keyboard.

I tell stories for a living with video, stills, and drones. And I never book a shoot on Friday mornings if I can help it because, on Friday mornings at sunrise, you can always catch me in the lineup."

Marci Klein Comparing Surfing to Entrepreneurship:

1. Every time you fall, get back up. There is no other sport I have ever done that. In a manner of speaking, you fall off EVERY time and have to get back on the board, paddle back out and go again and again and again. What an incredible reminder for entrepreneurs. Growing up, so many of us are trained to be afraid of trying things because we are afraid to fail. As entrepreneurs, it is exactly the opposite, as with surfing – it is expected that you will fall off over and over again. Very quickly, it teaches us to try things and be ok with risk and failure. It becomes second nature and shows us that failure leads to learning and opportunity, which then leads to improvement and success. As entrepreneurs, it is no different. We are told NO over and over again, and it requires inner confidence, strength, and certainty to keep going, adapting, adjusting, learning, and getting back up and going again.

2. Surfing, like entrepreneurship, is a spiritual journey. When I was younger, I looked at surfing through a different lens. It was something I did for fun, adventure, travel, and a fantastic workout. But as I have matured, and spent most of my life in the water, I see it as so much more; it's a spiritual experience that never stops astounding me. Being part of nature, paddling out there with all types of ocean life – great white sharks included – witnessing wind, rain, sun, moon and all of the majesty and danger that nature has to offer, it becomes a spiritual practice of trusting and being humble to mother nature's magnificence.

Entrepreneurship has the same magic and power. It requires focus and discipline and the ultimate confidence in yourself as well as trust in the process. As an entrepreneur, there are moments when you have no idea what the next step is or how you will get through. You just have to have the unwavering discipline, belief, and commitment to taking that next step and trusting that somehow, someway, it will appear. It can be the same with a wave that is bigger than you have ever paddled into, and you just have to breathe, fully commit, dig in and go, and trust that it will work out. Ultimately, they are spiritual journeys that will test your sheer grit, faith, and commitment, and in the end, there is nothing more rewarding or more worth it!

3. Mind over matter. Our attitudes shape our reality. If you think you can't, you won't. If you think you can, you will. It is that simple. In surfing, if you get in the water and think you can't handle this or you are not going to have fun or if you are paddling for a wave and think, "I am not going to get this," you won't. I remember my first solo surf adventure to Costa Rica - just me and my surfboard. Aside from my first night's hotel room, I had no idea where I was going to stay, who I would hang out with, where the surf spots were, or how I'd get to them without renting a car (I was on a tight budget). But I got on the plane and figured it out almost immediately. The first night I met a couple of surfers whose car had broken down right in front of my hotel. The garage couldn't get the parts to fix their car till the next day, so I offered them the 2nd bed in my hotel room. The next thing you know, I have surf buddies, and a ride to the surf break I had read about in my tour book. It turns out one of the stranded surfers owned a hotel in the town of Dominical, and the other was a semi-pro surfer who stole my heart during the rest of my adventure. As an entrepreneur, it is no different. If we believe we are going to achieve our goal, achieve our dream, or succeed in our business, we will. I recently said, **"If you believe in the**

eventuality, eventually, it will become your reality." This has been my mantra every time someone has told me, "You can't do that," and in my mind, I respond, "Oh yeah, watch me!"

4. Be present. Surfing forces us to be present in the here and now. If you get ahead of yourself and think about the last wave, what you need to do for the upcoming wave, or even thinking about your to-do list, it can throw you off from being able to respond to the changes with each wave because every wave is different. By staying very present in each moment, you can adapt and adjust your paddle, pop up, stance, or otherwise to make magic happen. As an entrepreneur, there is always a lot of planning involved. There are also obstacles and opportunities at every turn. If we are present and pay attention, we can often look for opportunities to turn those obstacles into our advantage. If we lose focus and presence for one moment, we can be thrown off our game, just like being thrown off our boards. Rather staying present, smiling and rolling with what comes our way always lead to the long-term wins.

5. Ego is no amigo. Some people may argue that as an entrepreneur, you have to have an ego. But in the end, I'm not convinced this is the case. Confidence, yes; Ego, no. In surfing, you can see it when egos get involved; it ruins the passion, love, and spirit of the sport, and often fights break out. One of the most famous surf quotes is, "The best surfer out there is the one having the most fun." As I have been on the journey as an entrepreneur, when I look around at those mentors and leaders that most inspire me, like Richard Branson, what stands out is a commitment to authenticity, following their heart, and having fun. When things get tough in the water or out, I always remember this and take a few moments to breathe, lighten up,

Laugh a little and have more fun, as it always put everything back into perspective, and back on track.

6. Persistence and perseverance paved the way. Taking that extra paddle and making that extra effort paves the way for that pay off of that awesome wave you catch. If you fail once, fail twice, fail thrice, try, try again, and keep at it. Your effort will pay off. As an entrepreneur, this is key; if you take that extra step, persist, and persevere, you can't fail. You may "fail," but what you gain in experience, opportunity and learning will put you ahead of the curve the next time you get out there. So, don't give up, keep going until your effort paves the way for more joy, success, and excitement.

7. Camaraderie and character are key. One of the beautiful things about surfing is that it builds character and creates a certain bond that is hard to find elsewhere. Those tough paddle outs, long road trips, or just long lulls between sets bring out a side of surfers that few get to experience. Plus, the lingo that goes with it, "get barreled," "closeouts," "brah," "stoked," "shred," and "snake" (and the list goes on) or the pre- and post-surf getting naked (towel change) in parking lots, along PCH, or wherever, create a community and bond that is hard to explain and hard to find elsewhere. Well, except perhaps as entrepreneurs. Entrepreneurship is tough, grueling, and some days can be downright defeating and unrewarding. Yet, somehow, as with surfing, those most challenging moments or most incredible wins, the long hours or quirky startup babble, can build bonds that last a lifetime. The combination of the two – surfing and entrepreneurship – is an even more powerful combination to reckon with!

Back to speaking about "snaking" - Snaking is a "no-no" in surfing. That's where you steal the wave that was not supposed to be yours to the detriment of another person in the proper position. The person who takes the wave is the "snake." In our group, our inside joke is that we compete for the title of President of the USA (United Snakes of America). The worst offender gets the "President" title. The title actually carries a lot of pride and laughter amongst our group. I must admit that I have carried the title a lot more times than my buddies, and I wear the title proudly.

8. Patience pays, yet it's my worst attribute and always a work in progress. But I know it works! How many times when you are starting up your company and going after your dreams, do you want things to happen now and on your time? And it doesn't always – or usually – go that way? The waves are no different. There is nothing like sitting out on the water on a day when the waves, and sets, have a mind of their own and decide to come on their own time. You can get upset and frustrated that they aren't coming, or you can accept it and look around, enjoy the scenery, breathe, feel the wind in your hair, the sunrise or sunset, the dolphins, the seals, or the birds. Even the people chatting and laughing around you, can help you fully take in and enjoy the moment and opportunity at hand. (Or you can snake your friends on a small ripple and get in a good laugh. By the way, if you are not an experienced surfer, don't try this; it's very dangerous!) As entrepreneurs, we must learn patience. Surfing teaches us that over and over and over again.

9. Balance is the key. In surfing, it is all about balance, from lying on your board to riding with control, to managing your surf time. In entrepreneurship, there are many elements of balance to consider, most notably the work-life balance. I have two teenage boys, a husband, and a dog named Cody, friends, in addition to my own personal Zen time, which is surfing. It's so important to strike the balance that works for yourself. It's always a juggling act, but to me, that is what makes life exciting.

10. Have fun. There will be moments in surfing and in work that you hate the situation where you find yourself, but ultimately try and make it enjoyable. I always say that I have the best job in the world. What could be more fun than telling stories with the video? I am still riding a wave and having a blast, even when I'm sitting at the desk in my office. It's all about the way you look at life.

I genuinely believe that if you can successfully ride your own personal version of a wave, then you can successfully ride the wave of success with your business.

Who is Marci Klein?

Marci Klein is a 20-year veteran in the television business. An Emmy award director in the Director's Guild of America, Klein decided to open her own video production company after leaving the TV business to start her family.

After she graduated from the University of California, San Diego, with a degree in Communication Sciences in 1987, Marci devoted her career to the reality TV genre. She became a member of the Director's Guild of America in 1990 to work on Greg Kinnear's first network TV show, "The Best of the Worst." She has produced, directed, and written for some of the most recognized programs in television, including Fox's "Celebrity Boxing," WB's "Eliminate Deluxe," "Dr. Phil," "The Swan," and "Extra" and many others.

One of Marci's talents is on-camera coaching and directing. Her goal is to make her clients feel comfortable, confident, and authentic in front of the camera, which further enhances their brand story. Marci received many nominations and won a Los Angeles Emmy Award for a segment she directed on the Blind Children's Center, which was part of a 1-hour DGA sponsored project. She also received a Cable Ace Award for her work with the Los Angeles Fire Department.

More recently, Marci has also become a sport pilot, which was a huge accomplishment for her. Afraid of heights, Marci "went for it anyway" because she needed her pilot certificate to provide drone footage for her client videos legally. After six months of study, and training as a pilot, she took and passed the Part 61 sport pilot license, and Part 107 certification, which makes her one of the few unmanned aerial vehicle operators licensed to operate unmanned drones legally. She also has a rare night waiver that allows her to carry out her flying missions after sunset. Marci Balances work, family and philanthropy. She is a volteer for both her community and for non-profits. Marci is an Ambassador to the Redondo Beach Chamber of Commerce, a Public Arts Commissioner for the City of Redondo Beach, which is appointed by the Mayor, she also sits on the Board of Directors for both the Redondo Beach Chamber of Commerce, and Waterfront Education, a non-prfit organization that teaches kids to be stuards of the ocean. She is the mother of two teenage boys. She has a video production office and green screen studio just five blocks away from famous Redondo Beach

Pier, and only 15 minutes away from her favorite surf spot in Manhattan Beach.

Conversation with *Marci Klein, CEO of Klein Creative Media*

Tell us more about Klein Creative Media?

Marci: I didn't know it at the time that I started my video production marketing company, but video is 600% more effective as a marketing tool than print and Direct Mail marketing combined. Businesses who are not using video to tell stories are missing a huge opportunity to grow. But as I said, I didn't know that back in the day. All I knew was that I am a storyteller.

Klein Creative Media, we tell stories with video that create an impact while promoting company brand recognition without the Emmy price tag. I've worked on shows like Dr. Phil, Inside Edition, E! Entertainment Television, and I use that professional experience to coach and guide real people, not just professional actors, on how to appear on camera and represent their brand on video. I create brand videos, explainers, introductory videos, commercials, training videos, in-house sales videos, product launches, crowdfunding, and any kind of video businesses could need to help grow and promote their service and brand.

We can work from concept to completion. Many companies spend thousands of extra dollars on ad agencies, who then turn around and hire us to execute the project. We don't just produce the videos; we come up with concepts and scripts just like the large agencies, only we do it for a fraction of the cost.

Klein Creative Media is client-driven. We're collaborative, and we really listen to what our clients have to say because, ultimately, our clients want creativity, and they want out-of-the-box thinking, and we deliver that for a reasonable price.

I've always loved telling stories with video. And that is what my whole company is based on. We have our own camera gear, a small fleet of drones, and a production studio where we shoot anything from video blogs to commercials. With our long list of freelance creative crews, we also have the resources to grow and expand. Because of our experience and understanding of what it takes to get the story our clients want; we can provide excellent service at a fair rate. We travel to the location, or we shoot in the studio. We do our best to work with most client budgets and can work from the highest broadcast level to the small solopreneur business model.

Marci, the Video industry is thought of to be an influencer type industry, you know the "Who's Who type of World." What made you decide to launch in that arena?

Marci: I was working on a very popular TV show, (which will remain un-named) with one baby at home with the nanny, and one on the way. After working a typical 16-hour day, while practically endorsing my whole paycheck over to my nanny, I walked into work the next day and was yelled at for having left without "asking." That was my "Aha moment." It was in that instant that I realized TV wasn't the place for this mom. I wasn't willing to pass up an opportunity to raise my children, just to gain another TV show credit on my resume. So, I left TV and decided to be a stay-at-home mom. That lasted about seven years until the creative itch just couldn't be scratched with walks in the park and trips to the farmer's market for lunch. I wanted to create again…just as I did on TV.

I love telling stories with video, so in 2013, I grabbed a video camera and emulated the reality TV shows I used to produce. I created a pilot called "Court Kids," which was basically "Tiger Moms" for tennis. The tennis channel had an interest and told me I needed to incorporate to sell them the series. So, at their request, I incorporated, and unfortunately, my green light became yellow, and then red. The pilot never saw the light of day, except on my YouTube channel. But because I loved telling stories with video so much, I decided not to give up, but to use my corporate status to tell stories for businesses and real estate.

TV wasn't an option. I didn't consider TV an option at that time beccause I knew I wanted to continue to be an infuence, and take part in my children's lives, and with the grueling hours and inability to call your own shots in the tv industry, it just didn't seem like the right avenue. Still, at that juncture, I wanted to explore other alternatives as I still wanted to stay close to my kids. So, I started a small business at home, creating keepsake videos, short product videos, and real estate videos, then purchased a drone to take production to the next level.

Klein Creative Media has a studio. What made you branch out and extend your overhead?

Marci: Well, I was watching and waiting for the right wave long enough! It was time to surf! While I continued to work out of my home office, my kids decided they were tired of sharing a bedroom. This prompted me to vacate the home office space and look elsewhere.

Just a few weeks after my kid's announced they wanted me out, I happened upon a networking meeting where the office manager asked if anyone was interested in office space. Not thinking I would Have the guts to actually make the move and rent space - after all, it was just my kids suggetion, I looked anyway. It was too good to be true. Right size, right location…But…But what…But what if?

There is always the fear of the unknown and having my own professional office space was a scary thought. What if I didn't make enough money to pay the rent? My husband asked me the same question and warned me back. What if? Right?

Terrified, I went for it anyway and signed a 2-year lease because, by taking leaps of faith and going for it, even if it scared me, I always seem to figure it out and grow. At first, I ran all the equipment myself, including camera, sound, lights, and editing. But as I grew, I started to book freelance camera crews, and I took my regular place as the director, just like I did on television.

Within the first year, my business tripled in revenue. I was able to hire an assistant and start an internship program to teach young talent about working in the industry. Within the 2nd year, I was able to expand from just a production office to build my own green screen studio next door.

53

My favorite thing to do besides tell stories, is to use my personal stories of success and failure to teach and inspire the up and coming young video professionals.

Share with us, who is your ideal client?

Marci: My best client is any business that needs to convey a message using video and digital marketing. With my expertise from television and working with companies, I can produce videos that will do the job they were intended to do. This includes marketing video, professional television, or commercials. I also like to work with clients who need aerial cinematography.

Klein Creative Media's target is any business that needs to promote themselves and to grow their business using the powerful medium of video.

What sets Klein Creative Media apart from your competition?

Marci: Competition? Most of my competition in the South Bay is on my speed dial. They are my friends, and they are my business associates. We have hired each other for various jobs, and we collaborate to help each other's clients. I learned a long time ago that working together; we will help each other to flourish.

But what sets Klein Creative Media apart from other production companies, I believe, is our brand, which starts with me. I have passion, confidence, and excitement, about every video I produce. When meeting with potential clients, I think they can see the wheels in my head turning. I can't' help but throw out creative ideas and inspire them to want to go deeper with their story than they had imagined.

When a business decides to create video content, it's vital for them to feel comfortable with the person at the helm of their production. If the client and I connect, it's going to be a great experience. There will always be differences of creative opinions because every video is like creating a piece of art - it's subjective. It also boils down to good communication with the client during pre-production to make sure we are on the same page. If we veer off, I use open and honest conversations to get us back on track. My ego is at the door. I am always expecting changes. Sometimes there are very few changes, and sometimes there could be more substantial revisions. The whole idea of storytelling is a process. Cultivating long-lasting relationships with our clients is what Klein Creative Media is all about. I bring my energy, my enthusiasm, my various skills, and I always give a hundred and ten percent to every production, no matter its size.

Everyone perceives success differently. What makes you feel successful?

Marci: When people talk about the companies being successful, of course, the first thing I always think about is the financial aspect, making millions. And of course, no one goes into business to not make money. But to me, success is not only about the dollar signs.

To me, success is creating the ability to make choices; the projects I work on, if I go flying today, do I get aerial drone shots today, do I surf today, or do I spend quality time with my family today. Having those options is also something I think about as reaching a level of success for myself because being in a creative environment requires finding creative fuel.

As a television director, I never had the choice to say no. I had to create on-demand. There was no other option. I couldn't play hooky to surf or take the kids to the park. As an employee, you just don't have that flexibility. But as a business owner, I can rearrange my schedule to be with my kids, attend the school events, or even watch the waves to gain inspiration for my client's stories.

Every industry has problems. Can you share with us what you see as a barrier or obstacle in the Video Production Industry?

Marci: Great question. I think one of the most considerable problems the video industry faces is that there's a perception that nowadays technology is so cheap. Why should we hire a professional to make a video when we can shoot it on our iPhone, or we can buy a camera and shoot it ourselves? I want people to stop and think about why they hire professionals at all. If you have a toothaache, you go to the dentist right? I believe people do best when they stay in their own lane. I probably could do anything myself from fixing a faucet to doing my own bookkeeping, just by watching a YouTube video. Still, I don't because I know an expert can do it faster, better, and with a more favorable result. Using an expert, I trust the job will be done right.

It's the same with video. Sure, you can point and shoot, but are you telling a good, compelling story that highlights your brand the way you want to be perceived? Is it conveying the mood you wanted? Does it feel like your brand? Does the quality of your video match your high-quality product or service? Are your shots appropriately lit? Should you look directly into the lens? How should you wear your make-up? What is your wardrobe saying about you; will the colors appear good on camera? Do you have professional sound? Will your mic pick up background noise? Do you know the nuances of editing? When do you create a music transition, when to use a graphic or visual effect, etc.? Do you want to spend two months editing when Klein Creative Media can have it done in two days? What's your time worth? We have over 30 years of knowledge, knowing what works and what doesn't in video storytelling.

We also talk with you about how you want your story to come across to prospective clients. Does it convey the right message? What's the feel, the emotion you want to evoke from your viewers? Funny, serious, heartwarming? What music will you edit with, and what visuals? We ask all the questions that the average business owner wouldn't possibly know to ask unless they were in the profession.

I spend a great deal of time in discovery, learning about my clients, products, potential audience focus, and the vision. When we go to the editing stage, we produce video that is of the highest quality for use in social media to television.

Where do you see Klein Creative Media five years from now?

Marci: I would love to see Klein Creative Media as a known brand name in five years. I envision an expanded studio, but with all the same high energy and fun vibe we have now. I see us providing our service to corporate Fortune 100 and Fortune 500s companies. I see my staff and sub-contracting network expanding to bring the top-notch talents to my project so that we offer even higher quality products for our clients.

I also dream about creating a meaningful documentary about a subject that means a lot to me. I am sending out signals to the universe to bring me the client who has the budget to let me create a masterpiece – and hopefully, it will have to do with women in business, or surfing. My two favorite subjects.

2020 has already started with a bang, as Klein Creative Media just won the Easy Reader Newspaper's "Best of the Beach" contest naming us the best Video and Drone Production Company in the South Bay….so the sky is the limit for us! Ya' never know….

What action are you taking to reach those goals?

Marci: One of the biggest things I'm doing right now is to develop and advance Klein Creative Media's connections with Fortune 100 and Fortune 500s. I'm doing that through my association with Women Business Enterprise Council, which was the best thing that I could have ever done. This organization has offered me priceless amounts of support and education. The networking has been extremely valuable and has allowed me to link up with various corporations and build my network of potential clients.

And let's not forget, I am continuing to surf and fuel my creative soul so that I can deliver my clients their stories in a creative and effective format! I continue to enjoy this wave in life, and even when I fall off, I make sure to get back on and go for another ride!

Contact Marci Klein

Email: marci@kleincreativemedia.com
Phone Number: (310) 990-4120
Website: www.kleincreativemedia.com

YOU DON'T KNOW WHAT YOU DON'T KNOW

With AMY REISINGER, CEO OF STEELFUSION CLINICAL TOXICOLOGY LABORATORY, LLC

To develop, thrive, and survive, businesses impose various mission statements, policies, and guidelines to ensure they operate in a fashion consistent with their beliefs, values, and moral fabric. Research has shown that mission-driven companies exhibit innovation and retain their employees. Companies must articulate their purpose or mission – why they exist. Establishing policies and guidelines for the workforce, a rule book if you will, achieves clarity of expectations, which produces exceptional quality. Unfortunately, these rules can be overengineered and underwhelming. Therefore, they will be futile unless they are widely known, modeled, followed, and executed. They should be integrated, displayed, and referred to as part of the company's culture rather than being read once when initially hired and then disappearing forever into the abyss. Often, companies are mandated by laws or regulations, some that are industry or trade-specific, while others reflect the acumen of the business owner.

The Science of Success

When constructing your policies and guidelines, at a minimum, keep in mind two essential codes – Codes of Conduct and Ethics. Incorporating these codes builds trust and security. They communicate to employees that your company is committed to doing business responsibly while establishing credibility with partner companies and consumers.

Fostering rules of conduct sets the tone for new employees while also generating positive peer pressure to maintain a high level of work ethic that is consistent with the values of the business. A Code of Conduct is a set of rules that outlines the norms and responsibilities for the proper practices of the company. Conduct codes should generally cover behavior that, while not illegal, is nevertheless harmful to the company and its clients. A public policy removes anything arbitrary or murky when dealing with an employee who consistently fails to behave in a manner compliant with the company standards. Even just one such employee can potentially cause significant harm to a company. However, straightforward, objective expectations for employee behavior will present a solid foundation for identifying and addressing this kind of challenge. This code is applied to convey rules governing dress code, cell phone and computer usage, expenses, licensing requirements, and client entertainment policies – the list goes on.

On the other hand, a Code of Ethics refers to well-founded standards of right and wrong adopted to govern the conduct of a group of people. It serves as a reference for corrective action, or even termination, for employees who fail to meet the published standards. A business can benefit from having a Code of Ethics in place, both to avoid potential problems and to address them when they evolve. When considering this, ask yourself what would motivate and unite your employees in a company culture consistent with the values you want to maintain throughout your organization. The Institute of Business Ethics (IBE) was created in 1986 to encourage businesses to make decisions based on ethical values. The IBE says there are three questions to ask yourself every time you make a business decision to ensure that ethics are at the forefront of that decision-making process. Whether you have adopted a formal ethics policy or choose to lead more informally by example, here are the three questions to keep in mind:

1. Do I mind others knowing what I have decided?
2. Who does my decision affect or hurt?
3. Will my decision be considered fair by those affected?

"Being consistently ethical and attaining the highest level of integrity, compliance, and ethics is the key to good business. The way you do anything is the way you do everything."

Amy Reisinger

Amy Reisinger, CEO of SteelFusion Clinical Toxicology Laboratory, LLC

Codes don't necessarily touch on matters of illegality, but they do address important issues that affect the profitability, integrity, and reputation of a business. When defining your Code of Ethics, it is best to keep it straightforward. Make it known that the company will not tolerate unethical behavior and conduct. Focusing directly on communicating specific standards and expectations of your company will sensitize employees to issues that may not have been obvious to them, while avoiding inadvertent, yet potentially harmful missteps. Try utilizing bullet points instead of long-winded paragraphs and avoid overly complicated legalese and meaningless phrases. Remember, the policy is developed for all employees and must be easily digestible, regardless of one's position in the company structure. Policies should address the consequences of violating the code and how to report them. "Think before you do, say, or write anything. Is this true to my brand? Does it reflect my ethics?"

Modeling Desired Behavior

"If it's not modeled at the top, then it's not going to be executed at the bottom."

Amy Reisinger

An organization's strong moral foundation begins with its leaders. CEOs are expected, by shareholders and investors, to maintain high ethical standards. Although it doesn't always happen, today's regulatory environment makes it easier to identify transgressions and bring violators to justice. Research conducted by well-known Stanford psychologist, Al Bandura, among others, has shown that people tend to model favorable and desirable behaviors. Bandura defines specific stages of observational learning to include attention, retention, reproduction, and motivation. For observational modeling to occur, one needs to observe or attend to the model, remember the model's behavior, reproduce the model's behavior, and be motivated to do it again and again. Thus, organizational leaders must **practice what they preach** and be sure that they, themselves, are modeling the desired behaviors. If the highest ethical standards are desired within an organization, then high-profile leaders must demonstrate these standards and be beyond reproach in this regard. Their actions will often speak louder than their words when it comes to helping to create a more ethical environment within their organization. Organizational leaders should be mindful that they are being observed, and that others in the organization will likely follow their lead when it comes to ethical behavior and attitudes.

Breach of Ethics

Every so often, we hear about unethical and egregious behavior of organizations and their leaders. Confusing regulations, an endless supply of loopholes and details susceptible to illegal utilization; and the average person's inability to wade through a mountain of paperwork and medical verbiage, it's no wonder that hundreds of thousands of dollars are lost each year. There are several ways one can commit ethics violations, simply from just a lack of awareness. Examples include contravention of state and federal laws, fraud, tax evasion, deception of practices, conflict of interest, improper documentation, and safety violations. The commonness of these violations has led many insurance companies to issue a list of services to patients, encouraging them to report discrepancies. A robust ethics policy is encouraged and contains a fraud recognition and deterrence program, including, but not limited to, Good Laboratory Practices (GLP), validation and verification techniques, and adherence to the laboratory Standard Operating Procedures (SOPs) and promulgated methodologies. For example, a laboratory will report results that meet all compliance criteria - cradle to the grave. Historically, there have allegedly been "laboratories of choice," where clients took their samples with the understanding that they would receive the results they wanted. Hence, "deliberate" action or inaction allows results to appear as meeting all applicable compliance criteria when they do not. In today's world, there is another name, and it's called co-defendants. The CEO of SteelFusion Clinical Toxicology Laboratory, LLC, Amy Reisinger, urges other business owners to keep the moral high ground in mind when making any decision.

Deterrence of Ethics Violations

Improper handling of documentation can also be found in numerous industries. These include the financial, health, and legal industries. Many of the documents and files these professionals are responsible for contain sensitive and confidential information. When those items are carelessly handled or not secured according to standards, people's privacy, finances, and safety can be jeopardized. Ethical concerns in laboratory medicine have been given limited attention but are cropping up in everyday professional practice. Clinical laboratories have some unique moral anxieties, such as preserving patient information, retaining medical records, and collecting specimens, to name a few. Maintaining a Code of Ethics addresses matters that might occur without them. With deep roots in history, medical ethics encompass all aspects of patient care and research; the basic principles written by Hippocrates remain.

In summary, organizations can create a culture that supports and nurtures ethics, and good ethics equate to good business. Adhering strictly to a few important and easy to remember strategies can create and sustain a culture of ethics in any organization.

Who is Amy Reisinger?

Amy Reisinger is Chief Executive Officer and Toxicologist at SteelFusion Clinical Toxicology Laboratory, LLC. Ms. Reisinger studied Biology/Pre-Medicine at the University of North Carolina, Wilmington, Wilmington, North Carolina, and completed postgraduate studies for the Cardiovascular Perfusion Program at Duquesne University, Pittsburgh, Pennsylvania. Ms. Reisinger began her professional career conducting extracorporeal life support as an Extra Corporeal Membrane Oxygenation Specialist at Children's Hospital of Pittsburgh, Pennsylvania. She provided prolonged cardiac and respiratory support by monitoring patient hemodynamics and administering medications. Additionally, she supported the pathology and toxicology departments by dissecting and collecting pathological specimens for surgical and autopsy procedures and assisted in toxicology interpretations. She became a Research Scientist at GlaxoSmithKline, Research Triangle Park, North Carolina, where she provided regulatory support to the pharmaceutical industry. Ms. Reisinger is a Registered Histotechnician and Histologist with the American Society of Clinical Pathologists. She was responsible for performing gross and microscopic examinations of animal tissue, computing and evaluating organ weight data, utilized in toxicology studies for the anatomic and clinical pathology department. Additional responsibilities included: generating pathology interpretations for drug registration and safety assessment, designing study protocols, and training necropsy technicians utilizing GLPs.

Based on her knowledge of toxicology and pathology and understanding the logistics of performing clinical studies in accordance with GLPs, Ms. Reisinger served as a Study Director/Monitor at Bristol-Myers Squibb Company, Mt. Vernon, Indiana for GLP and non-GLP toxicology studies, including investigative and mechanistic studies. She prepared schedules for study activities; conducted data reviews; evaluated scientific data to develop conclusions derived from the studies undertaken; prepared reports and summaries of toxicology studies; prepared safety/risk assessments for human health based upon preclinical study results, ensured compliance with GLPs and SOPs, Quality Assurance, safety and animal welfare guidelines, and other state and federal regulations. Ms. Reisinger maintained knowledge of worldwide testing and registration requirements and initiated and monitored Contract Research Organization (CRO) studies. Additionally, Ms. Reisinger presented at scientific meetings and published papers in journals; participated in the investigation of complex findings encountered in nonclinical toxicity studies; maintained excellence in knowledge and evaluation group through their application in drug discovery and development; critically evaluated Human and Veterinary Pharmaceuticals; prepared Safety Data Sheets, and prepared Chemical Hygiene Plans for the safe handling of chemicals including test articles and formulation components.

Amy is published in the Journal of Analytical Toxicology, Neuropharm, Toxicologic Pathology, and Journal of the American

Association Laboratory Animal Science. Ms. Reisinger is also a member of the Society of Toxicology, American College of Toxicology, International Association of Coroners & Medical Examiners, Society of Forensic Toxicologists, American Society for Clinical Pathology, National Society for Histotechnology, and Project Management Institute.

Conversation with *Amy Reisinger, CEO of SteelFusion Clinical Toxicology Laboratory, LLC*

Could you tell us about SteelFusion Clinical Toxicology Laboratory, LLC?

Amy: SteelFusion ("Saliva Technology Excellence with Expert Leadership") Clinical Toxicology Laboratory, LLC, was established in 2014 as an independently owned and operated clinical toxicology laboratory to provide a distinctive method of drug testing that utilizes oral fluid. The bedrock of our company is the dynamic team of key personnel who genuinely represents a rare confluence of talent, experience, drive, ethics, and enthusiasm.

I purchased the assets of an existing laboratory, which included the necessary equipment and testing supplies, assumption of the Clinical Laboratory Improvement Amendments (CLIA) Certificate of Accreditation, but most critically, the analytical methods, validations, and extensive policies and procedures.

During our first year of operations, there were systemic changes in the clinical setting that adversely impacted the successful implementation of the original business plan. This resulted in dramatic declines in the rates of reimbursement for clinical testing, more stringent out-of-network limitations that were imposed, as well as subcontracted sales agents failing to develop new clients. To offset these difficulties, we were forced to "reinvent the wheel" by adjusting our business model to include additional markets focusing on forensic toxicology testing, judicial system rehabilitation programs, workman's compensation, and pre-employment testing.

We recognized the nationwide opioid drug epidemic was an area that was underserved by the current network of testing laboratories, and the ever-increasing rate of overdose deaths was overwhelming many of the nation's coroners and medical examiners. We ascertained that the predominantly county-run offices operate on lean, fixed budgets, and the dramatic increase of overdose deaths was consuming disproportionate amounts of annual budgets, much of which resulted in budgetary overruns and financial crises for many of the smaller, poorly funded counties.

In response, to better serve those impacted by the crisis, especially drug-overdose deaths, we developed a rapid and extremely sensitive method for the collection and quantification of oral cavity fluid samples for toxicology testing in post-mortem subjects. The development of this analytical method and collection procedure has led to an increase in safety for the forensic investigators, as well as law enforcement. In doing so, we created significant cost-savings for strained county budgets by reducing the volume of autopsies required and increasing the efficiency in determining the cause of death. It also allowed for a more effective allocation of personnel resources in the coroner's office, while providing an answer to the family of the deceased, as well as ancillary parties, including insurance companies.

Coroners and medical examiners traditionally rely on sample matrices such as blood, urine, vitreous, and tissue samples that require lengthy sample preparation procedures, which delay the reporting of results from weeks to even months. Our unique oral cavity fluid testing (that has been granted three U.S. patents, plus two pending, as well as a pending European patent application for 28 countries) supports key stakeholders by providing an economical, less time consuming, safe, and non-invasive collection method. The results are real-time data to the forensic and law-enforcement communities. I can reasonably say that our company is exceptional because we are turning traditional practices on their heads. As a result of our hard work and dedication to our principles and practices, we have consistently demonstrated technical excellence.

All of us perceive success differently. How do you perceive success for SteelFusion?

Amy: I have always envisioned and desired to create something extraordinarily simple that would improve the way we do things, both effectively and efficiently. By taking on the status quo, I have realized that some of what you lose provides you a chance to gain something better. According to recent data, this industry is being disrupted by our technology, which is driven by our low price and real-time availability. One of my ultimate pleasures is knowing our rapid toxicology testing has assisted clients in closing cases faster and, in some cases, even re-routing investigations. The testing also lessens the burden on family members, knowing they did not have to wait weeks, months, or in some cases, years for the results! Not only did we create new technology and service, but we have reduced the costs associated with it, which has helped to save hundreds of thousands of dollars for our communities, and coroners and medical examiners.

SteelFusion's continued success lies in our ability to be unconventional, yet revolutionary while moving the needle forward in the field of forensic sciences. We need to do the unthinkable, the impossible, and we have the innovation to make that happen.

"The obvious is that which is never seen until someone expresses it simply."

Kahlil Gibran

Being in the science industry, providing test results and developing new innovative technologies doesn't come without a price. Please share some barriers that you have faced in this industry.

Amy: I've examined this market and taken a hard look at the dead-end... no pun intended...conventions. I have seen that our industry has fallen into consistently suboptimal practices. Why do we put up with the same old, same old? It's simple! It's the "how we've always done things" mentality. Filling a gap requires a lot more than finding it. It requires an insight for a new way of doing things and convincing influential people that there's a better, more efficient way. Some of these people have enjoyed long and stable careers with minimal challenges to their authority, so they don't necessarily invite my recommended practices. Maintaining compliance, state-of-the-art equipment, required accreditations, and certifications, developing and implementing a marketing strategy, hiring and retaining talent, are all extremely expensive.

SteelFusion has made it our mission to educate communities, government officials, and other decision-makers to take the leap toward the benefits of utilizing our testing methods. We've succeeded by offering our first toxicology test free so that potential customers can compare our collection and rapid reporting to traditional collections and testing. Decision-makers are pleasantly surprised that our rapid testing methodology potentially saves them thousands of dollars, but most importantly, it saves them a priceless element - time.

Since you stated earlier that money issues could be an underlining reason for ethical violations, have you ever found yourself, as the CEO, in a situation where you had to make that ethical decision, and how did you handle it?

Amy: Unfortunately, too many times to count. All my decisions revolve around honesty and integrity that is the core of my reputation throughout my professional career. One that stands out is an opportunity of signing a multimillion-dollar Request For Proposal that could have established a solid foundation for achieving our goal as a company. After calculating the logistics and a bunch of "red flags" (and digesting copious amounts of antacids), I felt I was being rushed into a hasty decision. I knew I needed to take the necessary time to allow the truth to be unrevealed. The best advice I could give to someone would be to do your homework, investigate all aspects of your decision, and TAKE YOUR TIME! Finally, it doesn't hurt to find a great attorney, but most importantly, when your inner self speaks, LISTEN.... then run like hell! To me, conducting business without ethics is like a person having no soul.

What advice would you share with a young, future entrepreneur who wants to enter the toxicology industry?

Amy: The freshman entrepreneur should educate himself/herself and keep abreast of all current statutes, regulations, and other program requirements governing federal, state, and private health benefit plans (specifically including, but not limited to, Centers for Medicare & Medicaid Services). Rules and requirements for all personnel must be observed. Personnel responsible for the management of laboratories should accept that, as with other health professionals, they could have responsibilities over and above the minimum required by law. These standards of conduct are an integral part of the laboratory compliance and quality program. It is imperative that all personnel are familiar with these standards, and support of and adherence to these standards is an essential element of each employee's job performance. These standards of conduct are not intended to be moral excuses but an exclusive right of everyone to determine the honorable guidelines under which they live. However, these standards are intended to delineate the minimum conditions under which a laboratory employee must agree to perform professionally in order to continue employment with your company.

The entrepreneur should always promote the highest quality of care and adhere to not only the organization's policies and procedures, but also refrain from engaging in practices restricted by law to ensure the delivery of superior services. The company should not enter financial arrangements with referring agencies where those arrangements act as an inducement for the subject and its referral of examinations or the agency's independent assessment of what is best for the subject. Additionally, entrepreneurs should educate themselves about the severity of the consequences of unethical actions. The general principle of healthcare ethics is that the subject's welfare is paramount. However, the relationship between the laboratory and the subject is complicated by the fact that there could also be a contractual relationship between the requester and the laboratory. Although this relationship (which is often commercial) can frequently be perceived as the more important association, the laboratory's obligation should be to ensure that the subject's welfare and interest are always the first consideration and take precedence. The laboratory should treat all subject information fairly and without discrimination.

Finally, dedicate yourself to quest for a healthier organization by valuing integrity, leadership, performance, teamwork, and client focus with respect to your customers. When you promote the highest quality of care and model the organization's essential codes, you will ensure the delivery of superior services and create a work environment suitable for its employees. It will be a place where everyone's voice is heard, and issues can be communicated openly and resolved promptly.

A wise mentor once told me to "Be the best Amy you can be."

Barb Munch

"You Need to Know what you Don't Know.... Even if you Don't Want to Know it!"

Amy Reisinger

Amy Reisinger, CEO of SteelFusion Clinical Toxicology Laboratory, LLC

CONTACT AMY REISINGER

Email: amy@steelfusionlabs.com
Business Address: 1103 Donner Avenue Monessen, PA 15062
Phone No.: 724-691-0263
FAX: 724-420-5783
Website URL: www.steelfusionlabs.com
LinkedIn: https://www.linkedin.com/in/amy-reisinger-b59261b5/
Facebook: https://www.facebook.com/SteelFusionLabs
Twitter: https://twitter.com/SteelFusionLabs

Amy Reisinger, CEO of SteelFusion Clinical Toxicology Laboratory, LLC

ACHIEVING CONFIDENCE IN A MALE DRIVEN INDUSTRY

With LETICIA LATINO VAN-SPLUNTEREN, CEO OF NEPTUNO/SmartTecPort

"It's not about being one of the boys; it's about being a part of the team."

Back to the Beginning

Back in 2001, I did something that I had always sworn I would never do. I joined the family business. You might be asking yourself why I was so dead set against it. Well, basically because I knew I would have to deal with the fact that nepotism had landed me my job. And as a young professional, I truly wanted to build something on my own and walk my own path. So, when my father sat me down and told me that his strategic goal of establishing a footprint on the U.S. market included me, Leticia, as the boss, I had to stop myself from running in the opposite direction. Screaming. With my hair on fire. As someone who has always rolled up her sleeves and tackled the hard stuff, I didn't want a handout from "daddy."

So, it was not a surprise to anyone when I decided to join as Executive V.P. Very few employees, colleagues and industry peers attributed my new position to my many years of experience gained at top corporations such as Merrill Lynch and Nortel Networks. No, to Neptuno's other employees, I wasn't the boss thanks to my MBA in Investments or the master's in international business, or even because I spoke four languages proficiently.

My dad recruited and hired me: no interviews, no H.R. department, no trial period. Suffice to say my first days on the job weren't pretty. I have always been able to deal with tough stuff, but that whole transition was more than just a little blip. I received very little support where I expected it, especially from industry peers, and it felt, for a long time, like a lonely path.

"Imposter Syndrome"

It wasn't until I embarked on the journey of writing these words that I realized that I might have been suffering from what was originally dubbed in 1978 "Imposter Syndrome." In the book "The Imposter Phenomenon," the author says Imposter Syndrome is essentially perfectionism. This combined with an inordinate fear of failure, the refusal to take credit for one's accomplishments, and feelings of guilt about success. These feelings can be particularly burdensome to women whose success is atypical among family members or friends. A 2019 study showed that 66% of women had experienced it, compared to just over half of men. This syndrome has never been taken particularly seriously, surprise.

It now makes sense to me why back then, I allowed other people's opinions, and my own value set, to convince me that I didn't deserve my career. On the other hand, I understand that back then, a 28-year-old female executive had a hard time being taken seriously, especially in our very male-dominated industry.

Born into the Business

What many people didn't know is that I was basically born into the telecommunications business. My father, an Italian immigrant who arrived in Venezuela in the 1960s in search of a better future, understood very early the imminent boom that the communications industry was going to have. Without any type of engineering or college degree, he risked it all, and NEPTUNO eventually became one of the Leading Companies in the Wireless Towers manufacturing sectors in South America. With over 10,000 sites built and about 250 employees overall, that legacy is not one that's easy to carry on one's shoulders.

Luckily my father, at 85, is still a force to be reckoned with, and my brother, sister, and sister-in-law are heavily involved in our business as well, and we are really a great team together. I still cherish the memories of our Sunday outings, where we would accompany our father on site visits, and we would make our own fun by playing with the earth that had been removed from the tower foundation excavation. In contrast, our father, ever the perfectionist, was hard at work making sure that everything was going according to plan.

It is in my DNA.

The rebel in me resisted it (as all young people do at some point). Still, eventually, I realized that our business is in my DNA and that nothing brings me more joy, and I can't **find a** stronger **WHY** than to help expand my father's legacy and vision to the next level. Our family and our mission have intertwined to a point where we don't know which is which.

Changes happen giving you a nudge

Undoubtedly there are certain times in our lives when change is inevitable, 2001 was that year for me. I was in Miami working for Canada's biggest telecommunications group, Nortel Networks. The year before, Nortel had grossed US$30 billion and employed about 120,000 people. The prior 5-6 years were really "golden," and those who lived and breathed Telecom during that period would agree. I am grateful to have experienced it, but the decline was already on the horizon, and there were waves of layoffs starting to happen.

The realization hit me hard when I started seeing extremely talented people who had spent over 10-15 years in the company being let go from one day to the next. For big corporations, you are nothing more than a number on a ledger, a desk, a dollar value on a budget. As I saw many of my dear friends depart, who were all regarded as "top talent" at one point or the other, I questioned myself on the worthiness of all those late nights working without a break, or the canceled birthday dinners and missed anniversaries. It dawned on me that it wasn't worth it.

Taking the "happy meal layoff package"

If I was going to work that hard again, it would be for something that had real meaning and where the effort that I was putting forward would be to help build something that I could call mine. I called my boss and told him that I wanted to volunteer to leave in exchange for the "happy meal layoff package," as we used to call it. You might think, sure, big deal, you had your daddy's company to fall back on. Fair enough. But the decision was an extremely difficult one as I was on an H1-B visa that would allow me to stay in the USA as long as I worked for Nortel, so from the moment I "volunteered" to resign from my position in the company, I was given 30 days also to give up my spot in the USA.

To Nortel, I owe the best experience, my training, my work ethic, those precious connections, and so many true friendships. The respect that still exists amongst ex Nortel employees is worthy of a Harvard Business Case Review, in my opinion. We still feel the company culture and camaraderie even today; years after the company went belly up.

Countdown to exiting the U.S.

While the countdown to leaving the U.S. was ticking away, I had to be quick about reassessing how I would move forward. In my father's mind, I had to take some time off to recharge and reapply for a working visa now under a newly formed company, NEPTUNO USA, so that we could open our American office and start our expansion journey. I had a few problems with that plan. Although I knew more than the average industry expert about the specifics of the tower business, I was by no means an expert on the subject. I told my dad that I needed a full-immersion period, one where I could go to the factory with him and the engineers and learn what happens in the "field," not just at the office. I wanted to be able to really have an intelligent conversation about towers if I was to lead the U.S. office.

Negotiating the deal

So, the deal I negotiated with my new boss was the following: I was going to take six months off to recharge. I wanted to go live in France for a while so that I could perfect my French. I also felt that I had worked so very hard at Nortel that I wanted to reward my efforts by scratching a few things off my bucket list. It wasn't an easy negotiation (to him French is not the most useful language), but he accepted. See? **Pushing back pays off** even in family businesses. After spending six magical months in La Rochelle, France, I went back home to my beloved Venezuela learning as much as I could for a year and a half before I felt ready to return to Miami, with an L1 visa under my belt, prepared for the mission at hand.

Not incorporating for gold

One of the first things I did upon my return was to set up a meeting with an "incorporation consultant," someone who could be our guide as we established our corporate presence in the U.S. After a five-minute conversation, he looked at my father. He said: *"Well, Mr. Latino, the good news is that you have gold at your fingertips. You have a daughter. We can incorporate as a minority business, and that will provide you some nice opportunities right off the bat!"* I will spare you of all the "colorful" things that came to my mind as a potential response, but I was beyond offended and quite simply livid. The so-called "consultant" wasn't even addressing me; he was talking to my father like I wasn't even there! At that point, I told him that I hadn't joined the company because my gender represented "gold" and that we were taking "no shortcuts." We wanted to be known for the same reasons we were known internationally, out of the box engineering, high-quality products, and integrity. We left the meeting and didn't incorporate it as a minority. **BIG MISTAKE.**

Inroads from Scratch

So, I went off to make inroads from scratch, with no big company name on my business card to open doors for me (no more Merrill Lynch or Nortel printed boldly above my name), and with a razor-thin Business Development Budget to "test the waters." I knew that the task at hand wasn't going to be easy, but I seriously underestimated the challenges and dynamics the U.S. market would present. It is a well-known fact that the Gender Gap in the Technology Industry is worrisome, but what some people don't realize is that the Telecom Industry is lagging even further behind. This is probably the only industry when the line at the men's bathroom is never-ending at a trade show, and we women just breeze through ours. That sure feels great!

Challenges faced by Women in the Workplace

Women are faced with many challenges in the workplace. Pay gaps, less access to opportunities and favoritism, the "mom effect," investing gaps, exclusion from the boy's club, sexual harassment, and the list goes on and on. The challenges increase exponentially in male-dominated fields such as finance, technology, law, and politics. These sectors have 25% or fewer female employees, and an even smaller percentage of women in leadership roles.

According to research by Cornell University, "the difference between the occupations and industries in which men and women work has recently become the single largest cause of the gender pay gap, accounting for more than half of it." We know that the disparity between genders in the workforce has been detrimental. Still, research shows that an increase in diversity is not only good for the company but the economy.

The good news is that today's business climate is slowly transitioning from being male-dominated to embracing equality. But despite some steps in the right direction, women still face an uphill struggle in terms of proving themselves in disproportionately male industries. As a highly driven female entrepreneur, I understand these difficulties and have lived through many of what I call "interesting" situations, but rather than being discouraged by the imbalance; I have used it as motivation to achieve my goals.

The Numbers are Rising

A minuscule, yet massively interesting piece of data buried in the Labor Department's December 2019 jobs report found that women now occupy 50.4% of non-farming positions. So, it is safe to say that for the first time since 2010, women now outnumber men in the workforce. I never paid too much attention to data like this, but in the last few years, I almost feel a calling to help raise awareness. I have personally dealt with the age-old "men vs. women" fight, and I have always gone out of my way to praise the amazing men that have mentored me throughout my career. Without them, I really believe that my story would be different. The workforce is big enough for all of us, and when we all understand that by working together, we are more powerful and effective, we will become a better workforce and society as a whole. Meanwhile, I am convinced that there are still men AND women that take this conversation to the extreme, which makes it challenging to find the middle ground.

Equity and inequality.

I recently had a conversation with a man who was simply fuming because he had read an article about a museum curator who had announced that in 2020 the museum was only going to buy art made by women. He was beyond upset, and since he knew that I would be participating in this book project, he proceeded with his own version of the classic "you women need to stop complaining and playing the victim…" rant. At the time, I said that although I was happy that the museum was giving women such a big opportunity, I was also a little uncomfortable with men being completely cut out of the running. It is indeed discriminatory, too. After I got home, the conversation was still nagging at me, so I looked it up on our friend Google:

In November 2019, The Baltimore Museum of Art decided to make a bold step to correct gender imbalance after realizing that it had only purchased 4% of female produced art in 106 years of existence. So in 2019, to fix this inequity, the museum planned to buy only works made by female-identifying artists.

"This is how you raise awareness and shift the identity of an institution," museum director Christopher Bedford <u>told</u> The Baltimore Sun. "You don't just purchase one painting by a female artist of color and

hang it on the wall next to a painting by Mark Rothko. **To rectify centuries of imbalance, you have to do something radical."**

Hmm. Perspective is a curious thing, isn't it? Being courageous, like the Baltimore Museum of Art, is a way to get the ball rolling. We need to keep working hard to create equal opportunities for women in all industries. As added motivation, research now shows that having more women on teams and in leadership positions leads to:

- More innovation
- Higher ROEs and increased profitability
- Better problem-solving
- Increased mentorship and sponsorship opportunities

Experience is the Best Teacher.

The 20+ years that I have spent in a male-dominated industry have given me firsthand experience on how companies and individuals can take actions that set women up for success in any work environment. Here some of my thoughts and suggestions:

- **Don't let stereotypes influence you:** When women lead, their traits are often perceived negatively. Assertiveness is perceived as bossiness, and passion, and empathy as getting "worked up." It is crucial to change the narrative and that antiquated mindset and continue to lead with confidence.
- **Expand your network:** As a Latina with Sicilian roots, I have networking in my blood. I am your friend, coworker, confidant and cheerleader. I know I can call on you for advice, and my door is also open to you whenever you need me. However, even if you are like me and it comes naturally, but especially if it doesn't, building connections takes commitment. Network as much as you can within your industry circles and be consistent. **Strive to create genuine relationships** and don't use them only when you want to get something out of them. When I left Nortel, I made a point to make people know that I valued them and left gifts for my coworkers and bosses before I left.

Someone once told me that I networked with heart, and that has always stayed with me.

- I believe that it is only in recent times that women have achieved the confidence to unleash their own networking power and have realized that they are stronger together. I discovered this in 2017 when I had the chance to correct that big mistake I had made 15 years earlier. I made NEPTUNO a WOMAN OWNED CERTIFIED BUSINESS (WBENC). My advice to you is to find a network of women who support your goals, and you will be blown away by how many opportunities will start to materialize. Besides WBENC, I am also involved with Women of NATE (National Association of Tower Erectors) and the Women in Wireless Leadership Forum (part of the Wireless Infrastructure Association), and I find a great deal of support from my fellow Women Business Owners and other Women in Tech and Telecom. Needless to say, I am not suggesting that you should only focus on women related networking, which should be complementary to your regular networking activities. Some women embrace it so much than they alienate themselves from men in their field, and this is, of course, detrimental.
- **Set the stage:** Sometimes, when you're the only woman on the team, men may plan innocuous after-hours meetings or activities that alienate female members. And don't take me wrong; women sometimes do the same thing. Instead, set the stage, create the next situation, and **be an inclusive planner**. Don't leave anybody out.
- **Be patient with yourself and welcome failure as a teaching moment:** Failure isn't negative; it's an opportunity to learn, grow, and push boundaries that ultimately lead to success. Take a chance and fail. Try again and fail better, smarter, and faster, and remember that success takes time. It doesn't simply happen overnight. Be patient with yourself, and keep showing up to do the work day after day. **When you do the work consistently, success is inevitable**.

- **Own your successes:** When you accomplish something at work, share it with your team and your boss, and let others outside of your team know. Keep a journal that tracks what you've accomplished. Keeping your name and accomplishments at the forefront will keep you top of mind for new opportunities or promotions. Leveraging social media has also been key to my own success and raising the visibility of my achievements and things that I want my industry to know about. Gary Vaynerchuk's book "Crushing It" greatly helped me with this.
- **Learn to ask for what you want early on:** This goes back to not being afraid to fail. There are opportunities out there that might be perfect for you, but unless you tell your boss that you're interested, they may not know you'd like to be nominated. Ask, "what do I have to do to get to be a part of..." and then do it. The worst thing that can happen is that he/she says NO, and you are right there where you were before you asked the question. **Muster up the courage and go ask for what you want.**
- **If your company doesn't support you, find a place that will:** You have the choice to work where you want. You are driving your own bus. **Don't let circumstances pull you into directions you don't want to go.** Think hard about how you want to spend your days, what you are passionate about, and what type of company (if that's the environment you want to be in) you want to join. Is this a business that acts as a true advocate for inclusion and representation, and is it mission-driven? Does it align with your values? When you can choose where you want to work and what you want to do, satisfaction and productivity come along for the ride.
- **Don't be ashamed of being a MOM (or a caregiver):**
For both men and women, finding a work/life balance can sometimes be an elusive goal. One of the most challenging aspects of being a woman with the ambition to advance her career is to find creative ways to fulfill caregiving responsibilities (to both children and the elderly.) According to Journal Nature, more than 40 percent of women (23 percent for men) with full-

time jobs in science leave the field or switch to part-time work after having their first child. Undoubtedly, that has a direct impact on one's career trajectory. How parenthood affects the lives and careers of individual men and women is contingent on a myriad of social factors, including public and organizational policies regarding who is eligible for caregiving leave as well as cultural expectations about which family member should take on more caregiving work. Essentially whose career should be more important. Although it is common knowledge that fathers today are more hands-on that men from generations ago, mothers—even those employed full-time—still shoulder a disproportionate share of caregiving responsibilities.

Many mothers feel pushed out of professional careers by the lack of flexibility in workplaces, and by their colleagues' and bosses' assumption that they will be less committed to their work after having children. Even mothers who remain in the professional workforce full-time, encounter stereotypes painting them as less competent than equally qualified men and childless women. Mothers face salary penalties and career barriers even while contributing the same dedicated work.

When I had my first baby, I made the conscious choice that I would nurse him. It was important to me. I am fully aware that as moms, we all have different aspects of motherhood that we feel more attached to, and the choice on how to approach the task is unique to each woman, and that has to be respected. I was very lucky that I was my own boss. I had an office where I set up "shop" and would pump breast milk in between phone calls and emails. I was a 37-year-old first-time mom and ready to go toe to toe with anyone who was going to question my methods. There were times I had to slip out of meetings or take a few 'emergency' calls in my office because I had a schedule, and I had to stick to it. Efficiency and scheduling were the names of my game, and I was able to breastfeed both Christian and then Emma until both were a year old. I consider myself lucky because I know that most women don't have that same flexibility at work.

I am still puzzled by how in this day and age, companies in the U.S. are not required to have a lactation lounge or some sort of accommodation in this regard. Working moms in this country are often the subject of jokes or comments about having to leave "early" or not being able to put in the hours that men do. Despite these transformations, the U.S. is the only country among 41 nations that does not mandate any paid leave for new parents, according to data compiled by the Organization for Economic Cooperation and Development (OECD). The smallest amount of paid leave required in any of the other 40 nations is about two months, and Finland leads the rank with 14 months with both parents asked to share the time off in equal measure.

One thing is for sure, even when caregivers go to great lengths for their families, there is always a sense of "guilt" lying under the surface, hoping you're doing your best as you climb that mountain of "work/life balance." This is not an easy problem to solve, and while things hopefully change in this country, your best way around it is by working as smart as you can, delivering your work, and owning up to whatever stage of life you are in. Simply be great at what you do.

Think of what you need from your employer to achieve the balance you want. Do your asking and negotiate hard.

- **Be professional and develop a thick skin.** Yes, women in the workplace are sometimes treated differently to their male coworkers. If you work in a male-dominated industry with a boy's club mentality, it's important not to be over-sensitive. Again, using humor to let men know that they are making a sexist joke, or are asking you to do something they wouldn't ask of a male colleague, can be an excellent way to diffuse a situation while educating them that times have indeed changed.

If you want to be accepted and promoted for your achievements, and you work in a male-dominated field, try not to be horrified when you hear a swear word, for example. You don't want your colleagues to change the subject when you approach it. **It's not about being one of the boys; it's about being a part of the team.** And for this to happen, you may need to set aside your sensitivities.

A long time ago, when I was just starting out in my career, I had a ruthless male boss. He zeroed in on women, and his main modus operandi was intimidation. At a Christmas party, his wife once told me, "You know; he says that you are the only woman who has worked for him who has never cried." I hesitated at first, taken aback, but then blurted out, *"Oh, trust me, I've cried plenty. I have just done it inside a bathroom stall without anyone around to see me."*

You will encounter situations that will weaken you and play with your emotions. That's OK. Just remember that there are a time and place for everything. Every time I watch the Tom Hanks movie "A League of their Own" that famous scene in it, "There's no crying in baseball" takes me back to that memory. Try to protect your professional image as much as you can. As women, we will never break the "emotional stereotype" if we put our emotions front and center when someone makes us uncomfortable. Instead, let's **be more emotionally intelligent**, knowing when we can or can't bend that professional mindset and whether we should let those emotions come into the mix.

Now, it's also equally important to know when to say, "that's inappropriate." You have every right to be treated as a professional and respected at your job. And to get there, you must be willing to stick up for yourself. Act, speak, and carry yourself in the way you want and expect to be treated. **Cultivate your executive presence.**

In a mostly male field, there will always be critics and people who cross the line. You mustn't let this stop you from going after what you want and focusing on building your career. At the same time, remember that the professional and personal lines are very blurry sometimes, and you need to stick to your values and ethics to garner rock-solid respect and reputation. You have to **keep it professional at all times.**

Needless to say, if someone crosses the line, you need to act right away, call it out and report the behavior immediately.

Get Out of Your Comfort Zone on a Journey of Self-Discovery

On a more personal note, I am a firm believer in being on a constant journey of self-discovery. I am usually finding ways to disrupt myself and get out of my comfort zone. My dad always tells me that when I was younger, I would go to him and say, *"Daddy, you know what I was thinking?"* He claims that whenever I'd ask that simple question, he'd start trembling in his Italian leather loafers because once one of my crazy ideas came out of my mouth, he knew that I would want to pursue it no holds barred. That is something that has never changed.

This very book is part of one of those crazy ideas. Besides the cathartic value of writing this chapter, I can't begin to tell you the fantastic friendships and sisterhood that have been created with each one of the amazing women you are reading about in these pages. I said, "yes" to this project to get out of my comfort zone, and yet the outcome has blown me away. Any expectation I had has been repaid a thousand-fold with a prism-like result. **Don't do things because you expect something to happen. Do things because the idea of "doing it" gives you butterflies.**

Freeing the Butterflies

Back at the end of 2018, I would get those butterflies when I thought about hosting my own podcast show. I didn't have experience with anything like it, but I was already an avid fan of podcasts and loved all the original and, in a way, "raw" content that was now available to me.

I had been following Marketing Guru, Seth Godin, for quite a while. If you are not familiar with his work, I highly recommend that you check him out and sign up for his blog.)

I got an email about The Podcast Fellowship and how you could launch your own podcast in just one month. I didn't sign up right away. I hesitated for a few days and tried to dismiss the "butterflies" every time they would rear their heads, clamoring to be heard. Why do we do that? I don't know, but we all do. That's when you need to step it up, fight the fear and just do it.

My podcast, **Back2Basics Reconnecting to the essence of you,** has been "on the air" and streaming in all podcasting platforms since January 2019 and has been downloaded in every continent. By no means is it viral, but apparently there are people besides my husband that enjoy it and listen to it regularly.

What prompted me to do it is the idea that we spend our hours 'connected,' but we're drifting away from real human connection, especially to ourselves. In each episode, I have inspirational guests share the ways they stay true to their essence, their definite purpose, and what makes them TICK. The whole experience has been fulfilling beyond imagination, and the quality of people I have met through it is unparalleled.

Committing to a path of self-discovery will not only make you feel more fulfilled and help you live life more joyfully, but it will also help you develop traits and habits that will help you succeed in whatever you set your mind to. Regardless, if you are in the corporate world or your own entrepreneurial mission, these traits will smooth your path as you walk through it:

1. Cultivate confidence.

Be assertive. Being heard in male-dominated industries sometimes means learning not to allow others to speak over you or interrupt you. That doesn't mean you need to adopt rude behaviors and interrupt others, but it does sometimes mean insisting on having your say.

2. Stay positive.

A positive attitude, a big smile, and the disposition to say YES, without compromising your opinions or beliefs, of course, will go a long way. Conviction in your vision and ideas is also vital, especially if you are starting a new business. Most people will tell you that it won't work before they even give you a full chance to explain your vision. Stay away from naysayers and surround yourself with people that lift you up instead of tearing you down. Joining a Mastermind group - a peer-to-peer mentoring concept used to help members solve their problems with input and advice from the other group members - can be tremendously empowering and a great help in keeping up your perseverance and positive outlook on things.

3. Nourish a strong Work Ethic

Although there's not a universal definition, a strong work ethic encompasses key personality characteristics that dictate how you respond to certain circumstances. Honesty, integrity, humility, accountability, and self-discipline are among these essential traits which are indeed useful in every area of life, but more so if you are representing your employer in any capacity. Although most people acknowledge the importance of a strong work ethic, very few do something to strengthen it, and it can be a huge differentiator in the workplace.

4. Be Self-Motivated:

A 'go-getter' attitude shows initiative and is a leader's vital attribute. For every issue that you highlight, be ready to propose a solution or a plan of action. Don't wait to be told; being proactive shows that you can fit efficiently into an organizational structure without the need for constant supervision. It also shows reliability, commitment, and, yes, ambition!

5. Be an aggressive lifelong learner.

Curiosity makes you smarter. Be hungry to learn new things, to keep on top of the news in your specialty area and to become a Subject Matter expert in what you are passionate about. Take advantage of every relevant seminar and continuing education class you can. Stay on your toes. Being informed will help build your confidence, and you'll be a valuable resource to your organization.

6. Care about being respected more than being liked.

If a consistent, impulsive "sorry" is part of your go-to set of immediate responses to a disagreement, banish it from your vocabulary. Don't be a pleaser. Most believe that saying "sorry" too much can undermine their communication, and a significant minority think it's best not to use the word at all. In the corporate world, those who are constantly trying to appease others are often more likely to be trampled on than appreciated. When you are at fault, own up to it and apologize. However, don't be apologetic as a default.

7. Learn how to handle conflict.

This doesn't mean being combative. Nor does it mean constantly seeking to avoid conflict. When a conflict pops up, try to be forward-looking and empathetic, "so how do we move past this?" Listening is key to successful communication. My dad usually tells me, "You have two ears and one mouth, use them in the same proportion!" Yes, I'm a talker. Don't attack other people personally, ever, and don't let them attack you. Try putting yourself in the other person's shoes to gain perspective. Stay focused on the issue at hand. Be very careful not to email when you're angry or read emotion or tone into emails when it's not there. Don't hold a grudge and don't lose sight of the bigger picture. Being strategic in how you communicate is a must if you want to succeed.

8. Be generous and pay it forward

We are living in strange times. Rarely do you see people doing something nice for another without an ulterior motive? We are often angrier than kind. Anyone who is a frequent traveler can attest to that. I believe that an airplane boarding process depicts our current human state. When generosity happens, we show we care, and we start building trust, which is the foundation of any meaningful connection. A pay-it-forward attitude can become a career catalyst, because we live in a small world, and sooner or later, all our actions, positive or negative, will converge in the ultimate version of who we become. I have found great joy and gratification in mentoring younger women who are starting in the Telecom Industry. It just feels good to take the time to guide them and brainstorm with them about their dreams, goals, and hopes, and to design a path to achieve them. Although I never had official mentors, I am forever grateful to the men and women who were generous enough to share their time, knowledge, and connections with me to help me advance. Make sure you acknowledge your supporters. **Kind hearts are hard to find. Recognize them, and cherish them with all you've got.**

My Journey to Success is in this Chapter

As I write about my journey in these pages, it has prompted me to question my own success. I don't honestly measure my success by wealth, fame, or power. I reminisce about how far I've come. Looking back at individual projects or situations, I now know that trying my best, regardless of success or failure, was my achievement. And yet I have had moments that I have felt a complete failure, that I have been angry at life and circumstances, that I've had people I "trusted" screw me over, and then some.

For the past twenty years, my family and I have had to live at odds with an extremely unstable political situation in my home country, Venezuela, which was also the epicenter of our operations. Fifty years of my father's work are "buried" there. We have had to manage a company under extremely adverse conditions, one day at a time. Looking at the big picture, it's a wonder we didn't simply leave everything behind, as many other business owners have done over the years. Instead of giving it all up, we decided to fight instead. To reinvent ourselves and our organization. To make our new headquarters in the U.S., I am proud to have led that effort.

Rebranding Neptuno

Since I joined, we have focused on rebranding Neptuno as an innovator in the industry. With innovation in mind, we patented a few of the new designs. We also developed an enterprise Grade Asset Tracking Software; we adopted a revolutionary 3D Tower Mapping technology and launched the 'next-generation site survey' which enables the creation of a Digital Library of the Network that is vital in Emergency Recovery Situations. Additionally, we founded SmartTecPort, a company that is at the center of the SmartCities Movement, and that will bring innovation to Small Cells and 5G deployments.

Sometimes ego is a no-no and holds you back.

Reflecting on why I didn't want to make the company a Women Owned Certified Business from the get-go, I now realize that I let my own ego get in the way. I wanted to prove myself, and it cost us. I took it personally rather than focusing on how it could help the company take off. It is hard not to be passionate when you work in a family business, and not making things "about me" has been a constant struggle for me. The WBENC certification has helped us gain an audience with companies that have diversity sourcing programs that dedicate a portion of their budget to working with suppliers owned by women and minorities. The "promise" of what might happen is still more prominent than the impact of having the certification has had so far. We are still working hard for the "home-run." There's still a lot of work to do, but I already feel the tide changing.

Tackling the U.S. Market

The U.S. market is a behemoth for a privately family-owned company like us. Finding the necessary funding and reach to compete on a national scale has been the biggest barrier. With massive target customers such as AT&T, Verizon, T-Mobile/Sprint, the barriers to entry are high and quite daunting.

Bringing diversity to the Telecom Workforce is also something that I have become quite passionate about. Not only because I believe that having a different point of view in our workforce is important, but if you feed off the same kind of thinking and the same approach to things, group-think comes into play and innovation gets stuck.

Women bring different skillsets and a different approach to issues that haven't been there in the past. Additionally, it is quite baffling that while we all like to have the latest phone and are literally hooked on technology, our country is suffering from a significant shortage of telecommunications workers. This basically means that while the intention is to make the vision of 'Internet for all' a reality by 2030, the current shortage in our workforce will hinder it.

Too Many People lack access to Broadband Internet

When one thinks that there are still millions of children that can't do their homework because they don't have access to broadband internet, it's impossible not to have a sense of urgency. In our industry, we all know about the "homework gap," and as I heard someone say: "it is the cruelest part of the digital divide."

Then if you add extremely adverse and unexpected conditions such as the Coronavirus outbreak, our reliance in telework, online education, telehealth and remote support services not only is paramount but it is our lifeline to "survival". By March 2020, over 1,300,000 Million students had been impacted by school closures and millions of workers had already started working from home to mitigate spreading. Can you imagine going through the COVID-19 crisis with no connectivity at all? No Internet, no TV, no video conferencing, no streaming, no mobile service and so on. If you can't, then you agree with me on the importance of expanding our Telecommunication workforce so that we can be better prepared to face situations like this. As a society we need to not only to honor the work our Broadband workforce does but also we need to promote it so that our youth embraces the critical yet exciting jobs it provides.

Telecommunication Jobs Pay Well

Surprisingly enough, the jobs the telecommunications industry offers are very well-paid jobs, that can place a young person fresh out of school in a great career path in only 12 weeks of training. So yes, one of my current missions is to raise awareness about the many opportunities there are in our dynamic and ever-growing industry, and we need and want both men and women!

Don't Give Up on Your Dreams

I've shared a lot of thoughts about how to deal with the corporate world, but I know that many women dream of having something of their own and becoming their own boss. If you are one of them, I say go for it! More women than ever before are becoming aware of the opportunities available to them through entrepreneurship. Women are open to learning and good at working with others, which are two vital ingredients needed to run a business.

Over the last three years, the number of women-owned firms launched each day has doubled. Women are now starting an average of 1,200 new businesses a day in this country, which is excellent news if you're looking to become an entrepreneur yourself.

The last few generations have helped bring more women into the workforce, into corporate leadership roles, and Entrepreneurship. We've come a long way. But that doesn't mean we need to sit back. We need to forge ahead.

To achieve success not only as a woman in a male-dominated industry but in anything you set your mind to, be ready to work hard every day. Keep showing up consistently. Never lose confidence or fail to stand up for yourself. Remember that you earned your role for a reason and that any obstacle can eventually be overcome. We must move away from giving ourselves the excuse that certain situations are the way they are because of our gender. Simply be the best you can be and dream big. As my favorite writer, Paulo Coelho once said: "There is only one thing that makes a dream impossible to achieve: the fear of failure."

Who is Leticia Latino van Splunteren?

Leticia Latino van Splunteren is a recipient of the 2018 Women in IoT award by ConnectedMagazine and has been featured as one of the prominent women in Telecom by TowerXchange, the Wireless Industry Association (WIA), NEDAS and AGL magazine. She was a finalist in the 2019 WeInnovate! Program promoted by WBENC-Certified Women's Business Enterprises (WBEs) to showcase their company's expertise in areas of innovation that are critical to WBENC's Corporate Members. She was named 2019 Revolutionary CEO by Aspioneer and 2019 Transformational Leader by CIO. She's an active member of the SmartCity Council TaskForce, the WIA City Networks Task Force, and was appointed in June 2019 by the FCC Chairman as a full member of the Business Development Advisory Committee (BDAC) and as the Chair of the Job Skills and Training Working Group. She is a regular speaker at the Telecommunication Industry Conferences and Trade Shows. She's the host of Back2Basics Podcast and the creator of the #Time2Reconnect movement. She lives in Hollywood, Florida, with her husband Don and her kids Christian and Emma.

Contact Leticia Latino Van-Splunteren

Email: llatino@neptunousa.com
Website URL: www.neptunousa.com
Social Media:
LinkedIn: https://www.linkedin.com/in/leticia-latino-vansplunteren-795309/
Facebook: https://www.facebook.com/leticia.latinovan
Twitter: https://twitter.com/letilatino
IG: @letilatino

KRISTEN BILLINGSLEY

RESOURCEFULNESS MAKES GREAT LEADERS

With Kristen Billingsley, President of Heavy Duty Bus Parts, Inc

"Redefine the possible."

Resourcefulness is often misunderstood. Some people believe it's a means of coping with deprivation, but this is not true. Resourcefulness is about optimizing what you must work with and being clever with the tools and resources you have at hand to get the job done. We call it; **'redefining the possible,'** and it is a tremendous skill to have as a business leader!

The most successful leaders are adaptive when faced with obstacles. They discover ways to gather information quickly to make well-informed decisions while shaping their environment to get a task completed with efficiency. To be resourceful is a mindset and requires pragmatism, observing problems, and finding practical solutions. Leaders are required to be mindful of environment change and have an understanding of all the resources they have at hand while retaining their focus to meet their targets and objectives.

Resourcefulness and Innovation

In today's economic climate, resourcefulness is one of the most important paths to innovation. Innovation is not just about creating something new but also assists in making older things that are already established work better. Just like an experienced mechanic can do wonders in repairing an old vehicle with just a simple set of different tools and their own ingenuity. We see this same spirit in the maintenance of large facilities — factories, buildings, and aircraft: those who service them may not always follow a manual, but they diagnose problems and figure out what tools and materials they have at hand to come to a resolution. Call it 'resourceful innovation.' Change can sometimes catch us unaware and ill-prepared. In those circumstances, it's resourcefulness that makes you flexible in responding and keeps you focused so you can navigate quickly. Resourcefulness is about leading change.

Being resourceful is one of the best strategies a business can have. In fact, living in the information age with the use of technology, powerful resources are literally at your fingertips. The ability to be resourceful is a skill that allows people to create solutions with limited means. While many people think of the need to be resourceful based on everyday terms of money, time, and energy, resourcefulness is obtained through proper mental, physical, and emotional health.

Solving Problems with "True Grit"

The ability to create, innovate, and ultimately solve problems can happen with some ease. It can occur through open-mindedness, self-assurance, the power of observation, and using creativity. It happens through persistence, through hopefulness, and by becoming proactive. Some may say having "true grit."

- Resourcefulness doesn't leave you in a state of procrastination. It is a state of being proactive and is telling you to get your head in the game. To play your hand. To take a shot, find an opportunity to find a way.

- Resourceful entrepreneurs look for the common thread in every situation. They're good at observing and recognizing patterns to discover the common good; they see problems and failures as lessons, an opportunity for change, for resolutions to ongoing issues that will continue to cause problems if they go unnoticed.

- Resourceful people realize that opportunity is not scarce – it's abundant. It's all around them – and can be accessed by anyone at any point in time. It is using the power of observation to recognize room for improvement and the most efficient way to get there. Resourceful people want to find the most efficient strategy that will help them attain the result with this highest margin.

- Resourceful people are willing to attempt different strategies to identify the best one given the situation. Figurative brick walls stop many people. They either do not have any solution or try one solution and if it does not work, they give up. Failure is a learning experience.

- Resourceful people have a sense of awareness; they have a sense of gratitude and a sense of intuition. Above all — resourceful people never stop. They know there's an answer, a solution, or an opportunity around every corner. They know that it may take time to get the answer — but their resiliency and patience are what keeps them moving to the next possible solution.

Taking your idea to life

For first time entrepreneurs, things are straightforward when you make your initial steps. Set up a legal entity, buy some business cards, maybe register a domain and claim your social media accounts - now you look and feel like a real business. After that, things begin to really pick up as you start taking your idea to life.

You might have a road map of what is necessary to get there, maybe a calendar with objectives and tasks. Pretty straightforward, right? Then one day, something comes up, good or bad, and everything you thought was necessary, and everything you thought you needed to do becomes irrelevant in an instant. It could be a significant opportunity, a legal issue preventing your progress, a death, a team member leaving - there are endless reasons why things don't always go according to plan. For some start-ups, this is the end of the road, as the obstacles become too much to overcome. However, those who emerge from these challenges all have one thing in common; they are resourceful. Adapt, change, and grow. Choose love over fear.

Resourcefulness is a necessary skill

Being resourceful is now an essential skill for today's generation of leaders. It is not merely a matter of doing more with less — companies have preached this for at least a generation. Instead, what's important is the realization that you can do more with less because you and your colleagues are more capable than you first believed.

Resourcefulness is a virtue.

Resourcefulness is not a means of coping with deprivation. It's a growth mindset and becomes a virtue that opens the door to more exceptional accomplishments. Based on my observations of what resourceful leaders do, here are some suggestions for being resourceful.

You must first start with an open mind. **"Redefine the possible."** Being open-minded about new possibilities is critical to putting resourcefulness into action. The leader who steps up and says, "Yes, we can do this, let's find a way." is one who can push colleagues to do things that some might consider impractical or even impossible.

Turn innovation inward. Resourcefulness is about optimizing what you have to work with. Innovation is not just about creating something new; it also applies to make old things work better. Like the earlier example of a mechanic, let's take it to a school bus situation. If a driver is out on a route and there is an issue with a part, mirror, seat, etc., when it arrives back to the bus barn, the mechanic will locate a replacement or order the replacement to get the bus back in route promptly. Resourceful innovation makes it work.

Choose specifics. If you're thinking of the bigger picture and a possible downturn, it may be tempting to consider ways to reinvent how your company does business. Adopting a realistic attitude about what you can do in the short term might be more productive. That is, think to revise specific tasks as well as specific roles and responsibilities. Processes and procedures can be revamped with an eye toward simplicity and cost savings.

Lean on your staff. Conventional thinking in frugal times says stop spending, but sometimes managers conflate that mantra with "stop doing." A resourceful leader doesn't stand still and is an active/communicative leader - encouraging staff to give examples while communicating a consistent message. They are having discussions about what the team and individuals can accomplish doing more with less and turn it into a pragmatic process for improvement. Lead by example.

Celebrate the lessons. As evidenced by the popularity of frugality in consumerism, people feel good about exercising their resourcefulness. But to encourage the spread of resourcefulness, leaders must set ego and pride to the side and have hard conversations about finding a solution. Leaders must share their experiences to help and improve others in the industry. If they see someone experiencing a similar situation that they have previously encountered, the leader can share their knowledge to help overcome obstacles.

Resourcefulness, while critical now, should not be reserved just for hard times. When prosperity returns, relying on one's ability to do more with existing resources and lead people to do the same, will be virtuous behavior.

How Kristen discovered resourcefulness.

Kristen Billingsley's resourcefulness was put to the test when assuming her late husband's role at the helm of their family business, Heavy Duty Bus Parts, Inc. A school bus seats and lighting manufacturing company, a family's legacy that has survived by being innovative for over 50 years. Many blessings, as well as some hard lessons, were learned and continue to assist her in strengthening her skill set as a leader, delegating and providing HDBP's team members opportunities to work on themselves individually and as a team.

Having the support of this team has allowed Kristen to follow one of her passions, health & wellness, linking the two industries together. She began KB's & STUDIO 308, now unified as KB's Community in Historic Montgomery, Texas. Capitalizing on the many lessons learned, Kristen has created a space for people to unite as a community and educate themselves on the many tools needed to help them on this human walk. Kristen stated;

"Grateful for every step that I have taken to be where I am at this point in my life. Even the sad, murky, dirty ones, they have allowed me to learn, grow individually, in business, and love more. I am better at being a parent, a leader, a friend, and in life because of it."

Who is Kristen Billingsley?

I am a mother of two kids, entrepreneur, spiritual warrior, a widow, born and raised in Conroe, Texas, and currently resides in Montgomery, Texas.

I obtained a BA in Family & Consumer Sciences, specializing in Interior Design with a minor in Art from Sam Houston State University. After being a stay at home mom for many years, I immersed myself into the school bus industry in the HDBP accounting department and later stepping into the role of the leader after the sudden death of my late husband, Brandon Billingsley, in 2014.

I believe in growth from the messiest of situations and like to call them f****d up blessings. In every unplanned situation, there are blessings sprinkled around. Look for them!

I believe in the importance of love for building community while providing a healing place for the mind, body, and soul.

On my pathway of continually learning, growing, loving myself, and others, I discovered the belief that we are all on a human journey of learning lessons and growing to bring us closer to our higher self, closer to our truth and living in our mission.

Knowledge is power – Knowledge provides outlets to enhance education and open-mindedness in small ways that produce more noticeable results.

Consciousness – It's not just the combination of food, water, exercise, mental health, and connection to our spiritual source. It's about the quality and quantity of these things and listening to the signs that we are given in every moment; the whisper or message, listening, applying, finding the balance, and having the awareness.

What is HDBP?

For over 50 years, the Billingsley family has made it a common goal to increase their knowledge of the industry while expanding the product line to meet the current needs and demands of those working to provide safe pupil transportation.

Started in '69 as a school bus parts and pipe manufacturer, Billingsley Parts & Equipment quickly became a well-known, respected name in the industry. With ongoing research of products and the market, the family unexpectedly changed directions of the business with the death of LB Billingsley, Brandon's grandfather. Don Billingsley, Brandon's father, later opened the doors of Heavy-Duty Bus Parts, Inc., (HDBP) in 1996. Brandon became the VP of HDBP after completing his BA at Southwest State University, and we later purchased it in 2006 (before he died in 2014. Remove please)

HDBP is a leader in providing direct supplier prices for original equipment manufacturer (OEM) and aftermarket parts. We offer same-day shipping on aftermarket parts along with outstanding customer service and online ordering at www.directbus.com. DirectBus.com was launched in 2001 as the online division of HDBP and recently got an upgrade in February 2020. We streamlined the process to make viewing our products and ordering more user-friendly. Not only can you order parts, now you will find an inspection checklist, instructional videos, and more.

HDBP is a proud member of WBENC The Women's Business Enterprise National Council, National Association of Pupil Transportation, and many of the 50 state affiliates; Texas Association for Pupil Transportation, Texas Technicians, Georgia, Arkansas, Missouri, Gulf Coast and many more, as well as, regional transportation organizations, We partner with School Transportation News, School Bus Fleet, and many more strategic partners.

I APPRECIATE ALL OF YOU - The HDBP staff, the customers, the drivers, the mechanics, the suppliers, and the many people working diligently for the safety of transporting our youth.

HDBP has decades of school bus industry experience through parts and manufacturing. We are a one-stop-shop for aftermarket parts, manufacturing school bus seat covers, and school bus lighting.

Our passion for student safety shows in the care and innovation of our one-of-a-kind products, with a portion of manufacturing performed in house and another piece being done with stringent quality control. We are currently working on our ISO 9001 certification, in combination with our computerized technological investments to our operation so we can turn custom products out swiftly. All the while, maintaining high production quantities and same-day shipping. We take pride in providing the best quality and safety while transporting our most precious cargo...the students!

We are the third-largest seat cover manufacturer, selling direct to school districts and also through a distribution network across the country. The workmanship allows for flexibility during installation as well as durability from the double-stitched seams. The customer is also able to choose custom colors and fit for the specific make and model of the school buses in their fleet. Also, we design and engineer a custom product line. Our wide variety of product classifications are offered at competitive pricing and same-day shipping.

Conversation with Kristen Billingsley, President of Heavy Duty Bus Parts, Inc.

Kristen, would you share with us your vision of success?

Kristen: Encouraging the community, men, women, and kids "to be the change we want to see in the world." – Gandhi. We are working together, learning, and providing tools to help us grow individually to assist in our success to manifest into success for the entire community.

As a certified Women-owned business, what would you say the benefits of becoming certified have?? been for you?

Kristen: Being a certified women-owned business has created a pathway for opportunities that provide our customers with better pricing and the ability to form a relationship for future business. It has expanded the opportunities to share my story, obstacles, and assist others in their growth as women in the business world. I believe in finding a balance where men and women are uniting and supporting one another, encouraging the next generation of leaders and making life a little easier to navigate.

As you have stated throughout this chapter, you feel being resourceful is a key element to the success of a business and its leadership. Can you share with us how being resourceful has helped you?

Kristen: After the death of Brandon Billingsley, my late husband, there was an inevitable restructuring that had to take place on many different levels to allow space for myself, our family, and the HDBP team opportunities for growth. We knew how to develop superior products that exist in the market, and we had to navigate the next steps. My father in law, Don Billingsley, suggested we "get back to the basics." Some of the best advice I have received.

As a smaller company, product development can be costly. We are asked to develop products and stock them immediately. At one point, we may have several projects going at the same time with no inventory and no time to procrastinate. However, these challenges allow us to be resourceful and willing to attempt different strategies to identify the best solution, given the situation.

This awareness provided us with the opportunity to reevaluate Heavy Duty Bus Parts and its processes, expanding on our core products, and to innovate new product development. We had to reevaluate our development model with some of our strategic partners to maintain flow. This is where proactive resourcefulness was vitally important.

As a manufacturer, costs rise unexpectedly. Also, products within our supply chain can become delayed or unavailable for various reasons. Our customers require their products to be on time and at a fair price point.

When a bus is down and is not able to transport, the mechanics and technicians need the products sooner than later to get the bus back on the road. We continue to find ways to keep our "product pipeline" flowing. Spreading our supply chain out is the best way we found to address this issue and is something we have been working on for the past several years.

Share with us what sets HDBP apart from others in your industry?

Kristen: The school bus industry has done so much over the years to reduce student fatalities, which is terrific, but we want to do more. We want to find new avenues of education for every person involved from the youth, drivers, directors, and manufacturers. All of us in this "bleed yellow" industry.

We work towards uniting us all together for the same cause, to improve student safety while riding the "Yellow Bus." HDBP works diligently to learn and apply new technology to better the record and stats of our industry as a whole. We also partner with the Texas Association of Pupil Transportation, National Association of Pupil Transportation and School Transportation News to provide scholarships for students and adults. The Billingsley Memorial Scholarship is in honor of LB

Billingsley, Brandon's grandfather, which that adds additional college support to graduating high school seniors. The LBB Memorial Scholarship, in honor of Brandon Billingsley, provides the opportunity for adults to attend and further their education at the annual conferences, classes, and trade shows. We combined these two scholarships to be awarded through one fund, The Billingsley Memorial Scholarship.

According to National Highway Traffic and Safety Association NHTSA, "The school bus is the safest vehicle on the road – your child is much safer taking the bus to and from school than traveling by car. Although four to six school-age children die each year on school transportation vehicles, that's less than one percent of all traffic fatalities nationwide. NHTSA believes school buses should be as safe as possible. That's why our safety standards for school buses are above and beyond those for regular buses."

We continue to utilize our resourcefulness for market research, customer development, and manufacturing products, which already cross over into multiple transportation industries. We focus on building community, creating and maintaining relationships with strategic partners to improve the safety of the transportation industry to take that 1% to 0. It takes us all, especially the passenger car drivers to be aware that the flashing amber and red lights mean, *to pay attention and STOP for school buses.*

Kristen, I find it is amazing as a mother and leader of HDBP, you have found time to expand your personal horizons and start KB's & STUDIO 308, now known as KB's Community in Historic Montgomery TX. Tell us, what is KB's Community, and what made you decide to open KB's Community?

After Brandon's death, we were in a state of flux, maintaining and rebuilding HDBP. Even with the fantastic support team he had built, friends, family, employees, attorneys, accountants, and numerous other team members, we hit a big challenge. I didn't know if it was something from which I was going to be able to recover. At that point, I became super resourceful and looked at different options of help, income, and exploring the possibility of selling the business that I was suddenly in charge of.

I am a "follow the signs and whisper" kind of gal. I felt this pull in a particular direction, a pathway into exploring another passion of mine, health, and wellness. I wanted to advocate for all people who are in a continuous search for new ways to unite with themselves and their community. I heard a property that I frequently visited was for sale, which led me to create KB's Make-N-Take, a farm to table eatery, health product and wellness center in Historic Montgomery, TX. which happens to be the birthplace of the TEXAS flag. Unfortunately, there were structural issues with the building. We officially closed the doors in Feb.2020. Due to these unforeseen events, we grew from a brick and mortar storefront to something more mobile.

I became resourceful and through following my guidance systems and aligning with the proper teammates, KB's Community, a newer version is evolving. I continue to plant seeds to grow the community. My goal is to aide with providing tools to assist in individual growth, healing, and loving oneself in our journey. I want to offer modalities which have assisted me on my journey to help others; those behaviors learned and experienced that have assisted me on my journey, especially after the death of my husband and what is my "new walk." KB's provides a safe place for all to find and add tools to their toolbox assisting them in gaining knowledge, growing within, and connecting to their our higher self.

What I am doing is striving to bring the community together I am doing this with HDBP, KB's, being a mom, a friend, acting in loving kindness and continuing on my own healing journey so that I may be able to guide others along the way.

It took resourcefulness to coordinate all of my responsibilities, jobs chosen and inherited, stabilizing foundations for business and organizing life in such a way as to be successful both individually and collectively. We all grow personally from loving ourselves, feeling beautiful/handsome, experiencing life differently and at a higher vibration. KB's

Community provides this as community, for everyone, male, female, adults, and kids. More offerings are in the works for HDBP and KB's CommUNITY. Stay tuned to all the goodness heading your way!

CONTACT KRISTEN BILLINGSLEY

Business Name: Heavy Duty Bus Parts, Inc.
Business Phone Number: 800-505-2300
Website URL: www.directbus.com
Email: kristen@directbus.com

Business Name: KB's CommUNITY
Business Phone Number: 936-203-2383
Website URL: www.kbs-community.com
Email: feedyoursoulmontgomery@gmail.com

Twitter Link: https://twitter.com/knbillingsley
Facebook Link: https://www.facebook.com/kbfeedyoursoul/
Instagram Link: https://www.instagram.com/kbfeedyoursoul/
YouTube Link: https://www.youtube.com/channel/UCEbG7NHfKZVJcUWTHt6445g

Kristen Billingsley, President of Heavy Duty Bus Parts, Inc

SAY YES, WITH CONFIDENCE!
With MARIANNE ELLIS, CO-FOUNDER/CEO OF CEO SUCCESS COMMUNITY

Confidence is the key ingredient to getting what you want. After 30 years as an advertising executive and coaching more than 500 women CEOs, Marianne knows that it all boils down to that one dollop of special sauce.

Who is Marianne Ellis?

Marianne is a renowned leader in advertising, marketing, business coaching, RFPs, and business development; she averaged more than $100 million in new billing growth in less than 18 months for two different national advertising agencies, DDB Worldwide and Quigley-Simpson.

In her career, Marianne has held EVP, SVP, COO-level positions at network, and independent national advertising agencies. Her award-winning, successful advertising campaigns gained her acceptance to The Television Academy, and she enjoys attending the Emmy Awards. Through her advertising experience, Marianne developed sell-side skills and then developed buy-side expertise as a Senior Partner at External View Consulting, where she was a consultant on RFP reviews for Fortune 500 companies.

Currently, Marianne is CEO of VEO Group, working for major corporations, Women's Business Enterprise National Council (WBENC- largest certifier of women-owned business in the U.S.), and WBENC Business Owners to help them grow their brands and their businesses.

She is the author of *"5 Secrets to Matchmaker Success,"* a WBEC-West Platinum Supplier Program Developer & Trainer, as well as a past mentor Ambassador. VEO Group is a Certified Women's Business Enterprise (WBENC).

To advocate for women and diversity business owners, Marianne started CEO Success Community, a division of VEO Group, to grow companies from under $1 million to $20 million+ in a membership-based model. According to American Express, 98% of women-owned firms *do not* break the $1 million mark in revenue. This situation creates a tremendous need to provide coaching to help these firms reach the next level. Marianne is using her proven experience as a current business coach at SCE EDGE Program to help rising suppliers.

CEO Success Community is *the* source for women and diversity owned businesses seeking corporate contracts with Fortune 500 companies. Their mission is to show CEOs the fastest path to increased revenue and growth. They have created a community of like-minded CEOs who support personal and professional growth to achieve phenomenal results.

With both buy- and sell-side corporate contracting experience, they offer a full suite of tools to achieve rapid growth for CEOs: Sales Accelerator, Conference Maximizer, Proposals & RFPs, Business Innovation Plan, Entrepreneurial Flight™ to $20-50 million+, and Private Coaching supported by their CEO Platform.

Marianne is a graduate of the UCLA Anderson MDE program and Start-Up School 2018-Silicon Valley run by Y Combinator (the Harvard of Start-Ups), which has invested in Dropbox, Airbnb, Reddit, DoorDash, Weebly and more with a combined valuation of companies over $80 billion.

A sought-after speaker, Marianne, has presented at Facebook, and events sponsored by Google, Microsoft, AT&T, and other companies.

She is a national speaker for WBENC *Building Your Brand & Winning Business* and a Business Lab Coach at both Summit & Salute and the annual National Business Fair—coaching CEOs on their businesses. Marianne was a key speaker at WBEC-Pacific Bold Success, The New Method Conference, NAWBO Propel, NAWBO Beauty of Sales Chaos, and other events.

Marianne recently won the 2019 WBE Advocate of the Year Women's Business Enterprise National Council West and 2019 Community Impact Award.

Conversation with Marianne Ellis, Co-Founder/CEO of CEO Success Community

Marianne, you have an extensive career in coaching. Can you share with us how you got started?

Marianne: My story began when I saw a fellow woman business owner crying on a couch after a failed fast pitch with Union Bank at an annual business fair. I had a dilemma. Do I proceed with my scheduled Pfizer meeting to win more business for our advertising agency? Or, do I do what I think is right and help her? Without second-guessing my choice, I canceled my Pfizer meeting, and we got to work.

> *Having the confidence to make that choice changed my life.*

My advice to the defeated business owner was to go right back and try again but with a different approach. I assured her that I knew how to pitch corporations and could make this easy. Quickly, I told her to go with three selling points and two questions for her next fast pitch. She was my first coaching client, and we were working on a napkin. I said, "Don't quit and fly home. Trust me." She did, and it worked.

Word of my good deed quickly swept through the WBENC Community. My winning impromptu advice was turned into a webinar entitled "*5 Secrets to Matchmaker Success,*" and then it became a workshop.

Before I knew it, I was presenting with Amgen, Disney, and many other corporations on how to pitch and win business. I was offered the role of WBEC-West Platinum Supplier Trainer for all newly certified CEOs. Demand for private coaching to learn my secrets increased and corporations requested my coaching for their rising diversity business owners to save and grow their businesses.

To ensure I was providing the best coaching advice possible, I went back to UCLA, my alma mater, and graduated from the UCLA Anderson MDE—Management Development for Entrepreneurs Program.

My investment in UCLA Anderson soon paid off when I was asked to help a CEO who faced a serious cash-flow problem. She had fallen prey to two enterprising men who offered to help her business in return for promissory notes to the tune of 49% of her business. The problem was she did not understand how to value her business; she was giving away too much and potentially losing control of her third-generation family business. Luckily, fellow WBEs (Women Business Enterprise) CEOs reached out to me at a business conference and asked that I help her out. I agreed to meet with the two people who were clearly taking advantage of a CEO down on her luck. It was a stand-off meeting full of tension, but I supported this CEO as she fought back and retained control of her company.

As with all good stories, at VEO Group, we reached a crossroads. We had to turn away clients, and we could not continue working non-stop. It was time to innovate and use technology to expand and future-proof the business.

This decision led to a big leap of faith and my newest chapter as the Co-Founder of the CEO Success Community. I partnered with Janet Lienhard, a fellow WBE CEO from Virtual Instructor. She had the online learning and coding experience with clients like UC Berkeley, UCSD, Rady Children's Hospital, and she became the CTO. Together we wanted to protect and grow our CEO's businesses.

To give us the confidence and guidance to launch our company, we attended Start-Up School 2018-Silicon Valley run by Y Combinator (Y.C.) My weekly schedule was intense: Monday online moderating our Tech Founder Cohort, running down our MVP-minimum viable product-and discussing our weekly progress. Tuesday and Thursday were spent at Y.C.'s offices attending lectures by some of the greatest tech founders, people who wrote the first lines of code for Weebly, Gooble, Google, and more. Then, it was on to lunch with Tech Founders. Every Sunday night, Janet posted our weekly results and, as a Y.C. Alumnae, Janet, still makes sure to post our monthly updates.

In November of 2018, we launched CEO Success Community, and we began by meeting every Thursday morning at 7:55 am on Zoom with our CEOs, coaching them with our Sales Accelerator Program to help them strategically and rapidly grow their business.

People may be unaware of the CEO Success Community; can you tell us more about this group?

Marianne: Our CEO Success Community is a membership-based community that promotes, supports, and protects each other's businesses. We are all certified by WBENC and are working toward growing our business through corporate contracting.

We are stronger together; therefore, we regularly connect online via standing Coaching and Accountability Zoom calls. We also attend Corporate Diversity Events/Business Fairs, where we promote each other via a CEO Showcase sheet and create social events to build relationships with major corporations. We share resources on CRM, websites, virtual assistants, social media, fractional CFOs, and more. It is CEO and peer-to-peer coaching that is designed to get results.

The CEOs who join CEO Success Community must be willing to do two unexpected things. #1-Use Stretch Planning driven by their Risk Tolerance and #2-Support and look for sales for other CEOs in our Community. By taking these two unconventional moves, success comes to you. Our approach is action-oriented, tough love. We coach and offer proven tools that have succeeded in creating long-term relationships with corporations and winning projects/contracts for years.

What's truly amazing about CEO Success Community are the CEOs who are members. This is a dynamic group of women business owners who came into leadership based on one of the following life events: 1) Adversity (death or illness of a spouse, loss of a job, lack of child care), 2) Confidence they could do it better on their own, 3) Inheriting a family business and now leading the company in which they grew up.

Every single one of these CEOs says, "Yes, with confidence" to grow their business. They push any fear out of their minds. They are truly an inspiration.

Let's start with Karen Mason, Owner & CEO United Transmission Exchange (UTX). Karen recently won Inspirational Entrepreneur of the Year, but she began as a reluctant CEO with no business management experience or knowledge of Allison Transmissions for heavy-duty trucks. As her husband, Tommy Mason, was turning the business around; he began to suffer the effects of head injuries he had sustained during his many years as an NFL running back and was unable to continue managing the company. Karen stepped in, and with the help of her team at UTX, the business went from struggling to successful. It is now an industry leader, and UTX has won awards from the military and is trusted by fire departments, schools, government agencies, transit, and utility customers. Karen is an innovative thinker and remains calm under pressure.

Karen: *CEO Success Community is an asset to our organization. Marianne has shaped our thinking more strategically working with us on how to position our company while keeping a focus on sales and marketing, always with a heart of gold.*

Marianne: Lynn Niewiadomski is President & Principal Scientist, EnCore Consulting, which keeps its clients compliant and inspection ready. The company has more than 25 years of experience providing environmental compliance and remediation, including investigation, site cleanup, emergency response, spill prevention, hazardous waste, and air compliance. Her business is both high quality and cost-effective. Expert in the Clean Air Act, Clean Water Act, Resource Conservation and Recovery Act, Oil Pollution Act, and Community Right to Know Act, Lynn sets a high bar for customer service and has developed a reputation for having the ability to do the impossible. She is an inspiration to our CEO Community.

Lynn: *Marianne has excellent coaching advice, no matter what tough topic I throw at her. Whether we are talking finance, employees, operation, pricing, or contract negotiation—she gives me the confidence to run my business.*

Marianne: Pamela Stambaugh, President and Founder Accountability Pays has 30 years of international experience coaching, training leaders, and facilitating strategic change. In large enterprises, her actionable metrics include an ISO 10667 compliant assessment for producing optimal results through people. In companies of 50-1,000 employees, her client is the CEO and his/her executive team for utilizing CEO Tools 2.0. Recently accepted into the Toyota Mentorship Program, Pamela uses smart strategic out-of-the-box moves to grow her business and has put a succession plan in place to ensure her legacy as a force for positive change.

Pamela: *To a Fireball, 18-wheeler on a downhill run, Wonder Woman — thank you to Marianne and CEO Success Community.*

Marianne: Mitzy Wilson, President Box Express Manufacturing, is one of the few independent corrugated box manufacturers operating in Southern California, and she built her company for when you need results, fast. Mitzy created a disruptive process to offer a standard box delivery of 48 hours and an overnight delivery with her exclusive In-A-Bind Program. Her company goal is to be faster than the other box manufacturers. Mitzy's company currently has 77 employees, 15 production lines, 500 clients, and 35 years of industry experience. When it comes to making it happen, Mitzy is the essence of "can do."

Mitzy: *Best year in business after working with Marianne and CEO Success Community. Marianne is like having 6 salespeople assigned to your business.*

Marianne: Cathy (Cat) Tank, Chief Swag Officer CAT Communications, offers marketing solutions driven by the power of promotional products. Her award-winning programs provide a measurable return on investment. Each marketing campaign is designed specifically so that her customers exceed their goals. Cat built her company through repeat orders from satisfied clients, and when they moved companies, they took Cat with them. Cat does superior work, and once she gains the trust of one department, the others follow. When she launched her business, she was raising twins and has been the sole family provider since her husband became ill. We have a shared background from our advertising days. Major automotive, telecommunication, and utility clients count on her. I rely on Cat to help show other CEOs how to grow their business and become invaluable organically.

Cat: *Gotta say again, THANKS! I love learning and working with you, Marianne, and the CEO Success Community. Brainstorming, the "OMG I should be doing that" moments, the Ah-Ha moments, and all of the inspiration. Great Motivator/Energizer every time.*

Marianne: Michelle Manire, Founder & President of Coast to Coast Conferences & Events, was the first women general manager of Doubletree & Stouffers Hotels. She has more than 25 years of experience, producing more than 1,500 events and provides event planning and consulting services that save clients, on average, 20%-40% by negotiating great deals, uncovering hidden costs and reducing financial liability. As a founding member of CEO Success Community, Michelle went from reluctant presenter to Fast Pitch Winner. She is tremendously driven, creative, and is currently working on Sales Accelerator to focus on her best prospects. The companies that hire Michelle are the lucky ones.

Michelle: *As far as Marianne's group, CEO Success Community, I love it! I can't wait for our calls. I have tried many mastermind and coaching groups like Vistage and Pinnacle. It's really what fills the need that you have. I'm pretty analytical, so my sweet spot is building on a foundation, laying one brick at a time, and that's what we do.*

Marianne is the best sales tactician I have ever met. Janet is our brilliant techy nerd that builds the infrastructure. Being a CEO can be lonely at the top. Everyone in our mastermind are friends, supportive of each, provides constructive feedback, and refers business to each other. What more could you ask for!

Marianne: Pamela Feld, CEO Triumph Technology Group, has future-proofed her business by pivoting from managing office equipment technology to Cybersecurity protecting offices from quite literally going dark and out of business overnight. Her motto is, "it is not if but when -- you will be attacked." That is why she has diversified into offering Cybersecurity Consulting services, including Security Assessments, Security Awareness Training, Dark Web Monitoring, Data Privacy, and Security Compliance. Pam discovered this new passion several years ago when one of her largest corporate clients had its printers hacked. She found this was not uncommon; in fact, 6,000 businesses were being attacked daily. Always a visionary and expert connector, she put together a team of respected industry experts, went back to school for her Master's in Cybersecurity, and is quickly becoming an influencer in the industry as well as a requested speaker. With some tough love coaching, Pam has gone from reluctant presenter to Fast Pitch Winner in just a few short years. Always active in the business community, she has gone from newly minted Certified Women and Minority-Owned business to being selected for leadership roles in her respected Association - WBEC-West. She recently graduated from the Stanford Entrepreneurs Leaders Program, UCLA MDE program, and was recently accepted into the Amgen Mentorship program.

Pam: *Marianne is simply the best of everything. She has this amazing talent for discovering the diamond in all of us, tweaking it, and making it shine. She has a unique way of giving you feedback that is kind yet incredibly business savvy from all her years of being on both sides of corporate procurement. There is no question that this is one of the most valuable programs for business owners who want to grow and scale their business that I have ever participated in. Not just theory and talk, but practical tips from someone who truly knows how to get the multi-million-dollar accounts with a proven track record. A huge thank you to Marianne and the entire CEO Success Community for becoming an indispensable part of my business and personal life. It is an honor and a pleasure to be part of this dynamic group.*

Marianne: Noushin Shamsili, Founder & CEO, NUCO Logistics, is an expert at domestic and international transportation. NUCO is an FMC-

OTI licensed NVOCC and forwarder that handles export and import shipments to and from the U.S. to global destinations. The company offers documentation services related to international trade and Incoterms. It can ship via ocean and air freight, tanker vessel cargo, breakbulk cargo, domestic trucking, all with the documentation required by U.S. Customs. Noushin took a significant risk in launching her business at the height of the economic downturn crash in 2008. Still, today NUCO has three offices across North America with agents in all major ports of the world. There is nothing that Noushin can't do. She is a smart, resilient powerhouse. Noushin is a recent graduate of the Energy Executive Program and was recently accepted to the Capital One Catapult Program to help transform her company to the next level.

Noushin: *Marianne, I have continuously expressed my gratitude for how you coached me and enhanced my approach in leading my company, but I still want to mention again as to how truly amazing you are and CEO Success Community!*

Marianne: Colleen Bonniol, Founder & CEO, MODE Studios, creates immersive experiences through architecture, media, lighting, movement, and interactivity. MODE transformed General Motors Headquarters in Detroit into an immersive Times Square showcase using a machine learning environment to handle the content for 17 screens. MODE has used holographic imagery to bring Alvin Ailey onstage to dance with his students for their 60th Anniversary Celebration. After graduating from Robert Half's Accelerated Leadership and Capital One's Catapult Program, Colleen developed an innovative new retail division for MODE. Colleen is the one who pushes our CEO Community to think bigger and bolder.

Colleen: *Marianne - after hearing you present Navigating Sales Chaos; I knew I had to join CEO Success Community. Thank you for all that you are doing for us. Simply put, you are amazing! I am so thrilled to be working with you. Confidence cannot be given to people, but you are certainly paving the road and handing out maps for those of us who need it!*

Marianne: Subha Rajana, Owner & CEO Biarca, works with CIOs, CTOs, and DevOp VPs to ensure that they are properly equipped for cloud migrations and projects. With Google, Biarca is both a partner, vendor, and visionary by becoming the third company to achieve its cloud security specialization. The Biarca engineering team makes sure that security and compliance always have a seat at the table. Subha, an engineer by training, envisions solutions to help her clients and grow her business—a real win-win. She is a recent graduate of the Robert Half Accelerated Leadership Development, Energy Executive Program, Dell Women in Tech Program, and is a pacesetter with our Sales Accelerator Program. She is a curious, continuous learner while participating in several executive management programs by both Stanford GSB and Tuck School of Business. She is a mentor, speaker, and panelist on various topics, including future of work, global women leadership, and exploring opportunities for young women in STEM.

Subha: *With Marianne & CEO Success Community's Sales Accelerator Program, we tackled the tough questions and built a pathway to dramatically grow our business. Her ability to help us quickly and clearly communicate our value is critical.*

Marianne: Ashwini Vasudeva and Sandhya Mukkamala, Co-Founders/Partners at Astute, are experts in enabling companies of all sizes to maintain compliance, recover lost revenues and increase profitability with their value-add certified accounting and business consulting firm. Headquartered in the San Francisco Bay Area, Astute advises Silicon Valley industries in the technology (HW/SW), semiconductor, biotech/pharma, consumer goods, power and utilities, manufacturing, construction, non-profit, and professional services sectors. They also serve growth-focused companies globally. The company offers R&D tax credits study, technical accounting, business process documentation, and helps companies recover lost revenues through royalty/licensing compliance audits, accounts payable audits, and time and expense audits. As one of the newest members of our community, Ashwini and Sandhya are taking a strategic approach to attend national conferences with our Conference Maximizer Program and ensuring their sales goals will be met with Sales Accelerator. They ask the tough questions of the CEO Success Community to ensure that value is being delivered.

Ashwini: *We count on Marianne and CEO Success Community to show us the way to corporate contracting success and enable other women-owned businesses to ensure financial well-being. Already we can see the strong network available to us, and we look forward to making the right strategic moves.*

Marianne: Monica Chung is Founder & Principal Broker, A.J. & Co, a top 5% San Francisco-based real estate firm providing customized concierge-level service to its clients. The firm's happy clients include employees from GAP, Stanford, Apple, and many more. Whether you need to rent, buy, sell, or invest, A.J. wants to be your Bay Area Real Estate Super Hero. I met Monica at an RFP Workshop that I led, which was sponsored by AT&T and California Water Service. Monica was fearless. She dove right into WBENC and wanted to understand how to best leverage her certification. No stone was left unturned. At the very next conference, she became a Fast Pitch semifinalist and went on to win the respect of the organization.

Monica: *Marianne and CEO Success Community were able to quickly help us figure out how to sell to Fortune 500 companies in the WBENC network, and we greatly appreciated her enthusiasm for our businesses.*

Marianne is my WBENC Success Hero. Thank you from the bottom of my heart.

Marianne: Karen Martin is the Founder & CEO of Pacific Planning Group, an urban planning firm that has evolved from land development services to promoting organic stewardship of natural resources, including land, water, and renewable energy. Its mission is to bring humanity into harmony with our planet's natural systems, which will create ripples of transformation that not only change landscapes but also the very meaning of being human. Four words capture the essence of the firm's process: "Discover, Imagine, Inspire, Transform." As an Urban Planning Firm with strong roots in UCI's School of Social Ecology, Pacific Planning began with a focus on permit processing, land entitlements, and preparing professional pre-construction reports for commercial retail clients, residential developments, and mixed-use developments. Clients count on Karen and her team for due diligence reports, site feasibility studies, preliminary site assessments and fee schedules, research and strategic planning, site analysis and title search, negotiations of development impact fees, land entitlement, permit processing, and project management. Karen was inspired after my training workshop to restart and rebrand her firm to be more aligned with her passion. The firm completed a restart in 2019 with a mission of harmonizing the built environment to be more in tune with natural systems related to water and energy. This mission promoted the move to UCI's Beall Applied Innovation Center. The Center is an ecosystem of idea generators, funders, UCI students, and mentors who collaborate to create a better world through social enterprise. Karen then strategically planned for her company's future by hiring a President who brings more than 30 years of experience in environmental, water, and energy management, positioning the firm to adapt to better serve its clients strategically.

Karen: *Marianne was my Platinum Supplier Program Trainer, and I gained so much strategic insight from her 2-day workshop that I transformed my business and my life. Marianne's coaching and her CEO Success Community not only highlights opportunities for all their members but also offers useful and authentic support and (dare I say it?) love for one another and the world that makes working and enterprise both financially and personally rewarding.*

Marianne: Kim Schmitz, President & Founder of Spin Event Management, whose mantra is "Events are about the Experience." She creates memorable experiences for attendees and strategically markets the events to increase attendance, awareness, and participation. Kim's offerings are based on four key elements that she calls IMPACT Elements. Within each of these IMPACT Elements, she identifies NEEDS to help their client define their event(s) and allow her to determine what is the right offering based on what they've identified. From sourcing, planning/executing and marketing internal/external meetings/events, user groups/conferences/tradeshows, to exclusive client prospects/events focused on lead generation, relationship/appreciation and awareness, Kim's experience and creativity really show from her commitment to her clients. You are in excellent hands with Spin Event Management.

Kim: *Joining CEO Success Community has given me a group of CEOs that are driving toward success for their company and mine. They truly care about supporting each other by sharing resources, leads, business insights, and more. Marianne impressed me with her sales skills and business acumen. Working on Sales Accelerator now to take Spin Event Management to the next level.*

Marianne: Kathie Tetreault, Owner & President of Saddleback Surveys (SBS), just announced that after 15 years in business, the firm is NOW signatory to the International Union of Operating Engineers – Local 12. This is a new and exciting change that Kathie is leading. SBS is well known and respected in the Surveying and Mapping Industry, having worked on Public and Private projects throughout Southern California since 2004. The company is very excited about this change and is looking forward to offering its services to an expanded client base. SBS has grown its services to include Geospatial Technology, bringing clients Design Grade Mobile Mapping, Scanning, and Drones. Kathie was open and excited to find a way to keep her company successful. The worst move you can make as a CEO is staying still. Kathie is focused on the future.

Kathie: *Marianne and the CEO Success Community have been so supportive and have kept me focused on the growth of my company. Being a CEO is a full-time job; it's easy to keep doing what you have been doing. Growth takes work, and through long discussions on the future of Saddleback Surveys, going Union was a smart move for us. I learned so much working with Marianne, such as learning how buyers read and grade RFP's; she is such an amazing resource. I am honored to be part of the like-minded community Marianne is growing!*

Why do you think your CEO Success Community gets results?

Marianne: It is a combination of tough love coaching from my days in selling/buying, a suite of proven tools, a community that supports and refers each other, and a reality check approach to business development.

When we coach CEOs to verify whether a prospect is a suspect, they always seem surprised. When we address a sales team and tell them to honestly share their revenue estimates per prospect to the annual goal number, the smoke and mirrors game goes away. Accountability is the key. When a salesperson needs to put her name on the potential revenue number, it gets "real" very quickly. Suddenly, the business in the pipeline receives a reality check.

Our drive to make sure a new business pipeline is real originated in how I got into business development in the first place.

Early in my career at DDB Worldwide, I was a happy account supervisor managing my current clients and growing their businesses. We had great clients, including Universal Pictures, CIGNA Healthcare, Wells Fargo, VW, Audi, and others.

Then one day, I was called into the conference room with the DDB management team. Something felt wrong, and all eyes were on me. The problem was we had lost a big piece of business, and if the revenue wasn't replaced soon with some new clients, we were going to have to lay off a lot of employees.

These employees were my friends. The crazy part of this meeting was that management thought I could help and that there were very few prospects in our pipeline. My track record of growing my current clients had gotten management's attention, and I had a high present-to-sell ratio. Also, I genuinely liked networking and helping companies grow their business.

So, I worked with the management team, and we created the rallying cry, "New Business Was Everybody's Business." We had all the employees reach out to their networks, to our suppliers, and to the community at large to see who was open to having us pitch their business. Understanding quickly who a prospect was (someone willing to change) and who was a suspect (not a real opportunity) became the way we determined where to invest our time and money. We worked hard at discovering quickly what the prospective clients needed, and even harder proving we were the ones who could deliver it to them. We had to win and do it quickly. We did, and it was indeed a monumental effort.

Today, when I work with CEOs on their business development pipeline, I feel as if I am transported back to that conference room when I felt like the weight of the world was on my shoulders to help drive new business into the agency as fast as I could.

Equally important, I have been both a buyer and a seller. Having the experience from both sides is invaluable. Working for DDB and Quigley-Simpson leading new businesses to sell advertising and communication services to corporations, you quickly see what is necessary to close the sale. Working with Clients at External View Consulting, you see how corporations evaluate new potential suppliers. Understanding what it takes to get a corporation like Allstate, Disney, or SCE to say, "yes" is foundational to the coaching we offer at CEO Success Community.

You were a private coach who extended your services and developed the CEO Success Community with your Co-Founder Janet Lienhard. Why a community?

Marianne: The idea for an ongoing CEO Community was a request I repeatedly heard after my two-day Platinum Supplier Program WBEC-West Workshops. The CEOs did not want the experience to end.

I saw first-hand how tough love coaching, coupled with a group of 15-20 CEOs brainstorming about each other's business, was the secret to smarter strategic risk-taking and provided the necessary proof to get a CEO to act.

After the Workshops, the CEOs would refer each other business and share resources. But over time, the frequency of interactions would reduce, and our sense of a united community would lessen.

This continued for two years as CEOs suggested creating group calls or in-person events in addition to my private coaching. They offered pricing suggestions and had the willingness to support me. But it wasn't until Janet Lienhard, a fellow WBE CEO, gave me a nudge. She said, "You could help more women business owners if you create an online CEO Platform, record videos to help educate and use the power of Zoom for CEO Community calls." With her support, I agreed to pivot and create a business. I'm very thankful for Janet's push, and Sue Berg, my ex-APS corporate client, in joining to help and grow our CEO Success Community today.

Marianne, could you share with us a few proven tools that we can use immediately on how to get what you want in business & life?

Marianne: Here are 7 very important tips everyone needs to know to be able to get what they want in both their personal and business lives! When you join CEO Success Community, we work on all of these:

- **The Magic of 5+.** 80% of sales are made on the 5th-12th contact. Use this to your advantage in your game plan with a 12-point Drip Plan to meet your goal.
- **Surround the Target.** Learn how to leverage the knowledge of the decision-maker, identify who influences that person and learn from who has been successful before.
- **Relevancy Grid.** Will your messages persuade based on how you package who you are and what you have accomplished?
- **Winning Presentations.** How do you present yourself and position yourself for the win?
- **Negotiations on Your Terms.** Pro-active instead of reactive.
- **Goal Setting.** Setting a course for your future 5-10-20 years out.
- **ROI Your Time & Money Investments.** You have choices, did you invest in yourself wisely?

What mistakes do you see women business owners make?

Marianne. Lack of Self-Promotion, Fuzzy Vision of the Future, and The Perfection Trap. All three challenges can be corrected once the CEO realizes she is doing it and has access to proven tools.

Eighty percent of sales are closed after the 5th-12th contact, according to the National Sales Association, so we make our CEOs show us how they have created 12 meaningful outreaches to their corporate prospects and referral base. This can include social posts, LinkedIn communication, emails, conferences, notes, phone calls, lunch & learns white papers, and more.

The problem of Fuzzy Vision gets cleared up right away when you apply metrics and weekly accountability. What gets measured gets done.

However, knowing when close enough is good enough is a major struggle for many CEOs. They strive for perfection, and this holds them back. Thankfully, our time at Y Combinator (Y.C.) Silicon Valley helped us learn when to push a CEO to go. When CEOs have the minimal viable product/service offering needed, they either should start iterating internally at their company, beta with their Clients, or go to the marketplace immediately to become the first mover.

As a certified Women-owned business, why would you recommend other women in business become certified?

Marianne: Yes, if you are seeking a corporate contract with a Fortune 500 company, government, or hoping to do business with other Diversity Business Owners, getting certified is a tremendous advantage. The certification provides credibility that you are corporate-ready, and it connects you to major corporations to facilitate business opportunities. Also, you are provided with education, training, and support. Finally, access to a network of fellow business owners, regional organizations, and national support is priceless.

Marianne, what is one piece of advice you would like to share with Future Business Leaders or a Woman in Business who is looking to grow her business?

Marianne: Say "Yes" with confidence. The Impostor Syndrome is a killer—don't fall victim to it. Believe in yourself. Do the work. Surround yourself with a community filled with smart people who know more than you and has your best interest at heart. Get a coach. Don't go it alone.

CONTACT MARIANNE ELLIS

Website: www.CEOSuccessCommunity.com
Email: marianne@CEOSuccesCommunity.com
Phone: 310.283.0726
LinkedIn: https://www.linkedin.com/in/marianne-ellis-28b81416/

WISDOM IN DECISION-MAKING
With PATTY TAULBEE, CEO OF PLANTLIFE

When this book opportunity presented itself, I thought of so many interesting things I've learned in business, but the one thing that kept coming to mind was decision-making. A slightly dry topic, but we sure like to watch and hear about other's experiences and stories, and if you think about it, those things are just the results of people's decisions in their life. So really, decisions are intriguing, and the more we know on the topic, the better.

I've compiled some insights that I've learned along the way that have been core to experiencing an awesome life, both personally and in business.

Decisions, we all make them, every day, all day long. Some good, some bad, some easy, some hard, but nonetheless, we all are faced with the same dilemma of having to make decisions in life! It's the beauty of our free will and our God-given right to make our own decisions and our own choices. Sounds "oh so wonderful" until we hit our early adulthood when the rubber meets the road and life happens. Then the question arises, am I making the right decision, and in those first years of independence, it's difficult to know, even if you have a sound support system. An early decision I remember was "what to do for a career." That decision caused stress throughout my life as I had no clear idea of what I should choose, and still don't to this day (that's a whole book in itself)!

An important thing to note is that decision-making has enormous impacts on every aspect of your life. Each decision you make has the potential to affect the kind of life you have. Making decisions is challenging for everyone, no matter their age, background, or economic status. You'd think with its importance and impact in our lives, that there would be more education on the subject.

Growing up, I don't remember anyone talking to me about decision-making, nor do I remember anything on the matter being taught in school. I do remember the swift judgment or ridicule I felt when getting it wrong.

In my opinion, correct decision-making is one of the most important aspects of living a successful life. Decisions mold who we become in life and, when not clearly understood, can have a negative impact on our lives and those around us. Sadly, our youth do not get the "life" tools they need through the education system. Perhaps this is why they do what they do!

Build Insights Not Regrets

I've made many bad decisions in my life and had to live with the effects. From the hardship and heartache those decisions brought, I gained a great deal of insight, which is a good thing. We all make bad decisions as we are human (just ask an older person what they regret), but the important thing is to learn from those bad decisions and not continue repeating them. When I was in my late twenties, after a few failed events in my life, I started questioning the choices I was making.

To me, a "decision" is the noun, and our "choice" is the verb. Our choices come from our decision-making process. If we never learn to make decisions properly, the choices we make will be the same with the same results.

Decisions and Choices Have Rippling Effects

Life has taught me that all decisions are important, no matter how small or insignificant they may seem. **Every decision you make today is your tomorrow.** When we make poor decisions, we must live with the consequences. When we make the right decisions, we get to enjoy the benefits. There are repercussions from everything we decide, and those decisions have rippling effects in our lives and those close to us. I've seen people's lives ruined by a simple decision that led to another and another going forward until the cumulative impact of that original decision had a negative outcome in their life. Just look at any person who is addicted to something, it all starts with one decision that was then repeated, even though the result was probably known or predictable. It breaks my heart to watch people make poor decisions that take them down dark paths and to wretched places. I'm sure you have seen this in someone you know or maybe even personally experienced it.

Get What You Want From Your Decision-making

The beauty of life, though, is that with good decisions, lives can be turned around. I've seen this happen many times. It is never too late, but it is up to each of us, as no one can decide and choose for you, again the beauty of our free will.

Our lives are our own, our decisions and choices are our own, and the results we get in life are strictly determined by how we make decisions and what we choose. People don't like to hear that because it's always easier to blame others or have an excuse if their life is not what they want or had hoped for.

Is Your List Too Long? Minimize Life-Changing Decisions

We don't put much thought into "what to eat for lunch" or "what movie to watch" as those are seemingly insignificant decisions that don't seem to matter much. Then there are those that we stress over, like "Is this the right person to marry" or "Should I change jobs." We consider those big decisions. I remember reading an article about the top ten stress-causing decisions, which stated that to maintain good health, you should limit the "big decisions" to no more than three at a time. I had over 50% of the list going on in my life, and yes, life was very stressful! I decided my health was more important and chose to table many of the things on my list. It's best to keep life-changing decisions to a minimum as stress actually prevents sound decision-making.

It's Your Life; They are Your Decisions and Choices

I think everyone can agree that life can be hard even when we strive to make the best decisions. We can't always control what happens to us in life, but we can control the decisions we make in response to the acts/choices of others. I grew up in a home filled with addictions and abuse that caused me to leave home in my early teens. If I had succumbed to what well-meaning people thought about me, or believed the prevailing academic advice on troubled teens, I would not have the life I have lived.

At 16, I made the most critical decision in my life, which set my course and caused me to realize my life was mine to live, my responsibility, no matter what the outcome. I decided to forgive, let go of the pain, forget the past, and move on. I do these things regularly to this day, as unforgiveness causes bitterness, which prevents us from living a happy life.

Don't be a Victim! Get out of the Rut!

It's imperative not to allow another person's actions/decisions to impact your life. I have many heart-wrenching stories of things I've experienced at the hand of another. Due to deciding early on not to let other people's bad behavior affect me, I've been able to recover and to keep moving forward in life, which has been key to my happiness and success. I often tell people not to let another person steal your peace. Sounds simple, but putting this into practice takes a concerted effort not to allow self-pity into your life, and thus, become a victim.

What a Person Thinks Turns into what They Believe

Like everything in life, learning and growing is a process that we all go through. It would be so nice if we woke up one morning and arrived at a successful life, but it requires our effort to decide correctly, to get there. Some people stay stuck in ruts and are never able to get out of them while others go from good to better. I started paying close attention to why this is so. In simple terms, it boils down to how a person thinks, i.e., thinks about themselves and thinks about their situation. In this way, **what a person thinks turns into what they believe, which affects decision-making at its core**. The record that plays in their head can be from what others put there or an accumulation of life events/results, but if a person believes the negative thoughts, it will cause them to become paralyzed in life. They remain in the same place until they change their thoughts and perceived perceptions about themselves and their life. I constantly guard my thoughts and refuse to dwell on negativity and emotions such as fear, worry, anxiety, unforgiveness, and bitterness. These things bring nothing good; they produce unhealthy decisions and can have detrimental effects on your life.

Logic vs. Emotion in Decision-making

Decision-making is difficult, mainly because we don't know what we don't know. I always wished I had someone to tell me exactly what to do, like following Siri's driving directions, "turn left and then right." It would be so easy. I don't enjoy making decisions that turn out wrong, especially when other people are involved. I've found that the outcome of any decision is more successful when it's based on logic and facts versus emotions.

Let's define decision-making.

I like Wikipedia's definition the best…"Decision-making is the mental process that leads to the selection of an action among several alternatives. Every decision-making process produces a final choice."

When I did a quick Google search on this topic, it was interesting…many definitions available from the business aspect, but what is business? It's an entity run by humans, and humans need to know how to make good decisions for their own life before they can ever do the same for a business.

What's a poor decision?

In a general sense, a poor decision is one that leads to an undesirable outcome. A poor decision can also be identified as one where you know you shouldn't do something, and you do it anyway. In this case, it will always be a poor decision. A straightforward example of this is eating something you know you have an intolerance to, and you eat it anyway. The result will always be the same, and you know it, but you do it anyway.

With many decisions, we do not know what the outcome will be. But if you do your due diligence in making the decision and it turns out wrong, it will only be a poor decision if you do not learn from it and repeat it. Albert Einstein is widely credited with saying, "The definition of insanity is doing the same thing over and over again but expecting different results."

What's a good decision?

A good decision is one made that has a successful outcome. You may not always see the result or success right away. It may take years to see it, but you will know it was the right decision as you experience its rewards. A simple example of this is working out! Say it's January 2nd, and you're pumped to get to the gym to start a Pilates class. You do the 1st class, and it's okay, a little sore, but good. You go again, still sore, and no real results. But if you keep it up, within a few months of going regularly, you will see that all that hard work paid off. It's that simple, and the same principle applies to all decisions. I call this principle "tenacity in decision-making."

Don't Give Up; Be Tenacious

I learned this principle from my dog. My best friend, a short-haired Dachshund named Buster (aka Butt). "No" was not in that dog's vocabulary. When he was a little, bitty thing, he could not make it up the stairs, but that dog would sit at the bottom of the stairs and instead of whine (a lesson in itself), Buster would jump until he made it and, even if he rolled back down five stairs, he would start again. He lived his life that way, which was always an inspiration to me. I often think of Buster during difficult times and remember that when the going gets tough, the tough get going…they don't quit! Throughout history, there have been many successful people who failed many times before they saw results. However, they did not let the failures beat them down. Instead, they got up, learned from it, brushed themselves off, and kept moving forward. That is good decision-making in action. **A secret to success in life is to learn from the past, but don't bring your past into your present.** It will weigh you down and rob you of your future.

In Business, Have a Process for Making Decisions

Throughout my business career, I saw the effect of decision-making in business. Some leader's decisions were catastrophic, and others were excellent. There is no crystal ball, and people are "only human" and make mistakes (just look at our world events), but when a company had a process for making decisions, it gave the company a clear advantage. The decision-making process that I observed to be the most successful was where decisions were based on facts and data, not ego or emotions. That took the "human" side out of the equation, which led to a much more significant win. I also observed the "team approach" decision-making style to be very successful. I adapted the team approach in my business, as it is the perfect combination of fact, data, and opinion.

You can be a Great Decision Maker!

People that know how to make good decisions are much more likely to be successful in all aspects of life. In business, it's imperative to be able to make good decisions and to know how to sift through what is important and when to decide. We often refer to people who make good decisions as "smart" or "educated," but in fact, no matter what our background, anyone can be a great decision-maker.

People often ask, **"How do I know if I'm making the right decision"**? There is no easy black and white answer to this question because every person and situation is unique and what might be right for you may not be right for me. I think that is why more teaching on the subject of decision-making is not available. Of course, people certainly will give you their opinion if you ask them, and sometimes they give it too freely. However, when it's a personal decision, only you can determine the correct choice for you. Each of us must come to our own conclusions and decide what is best for ourselves.

In business, you need to be much more in tune with external factors, such as the economy, global trends, the industry involved, etc.. The more you know, the easier it is to decision-well for the business. I spend at least 60% of my day researching to stay current. If a decision has a financial impact on the business, I complete full due diligence on the matter, so I'm well informed before moving forward.

Below are some **"wisdom tips"** that have brought me great success in life and business...

1. Watch and pay attention to what you think about. As a man thinketh, so is he. It's that simple. If you think you can't, you won't. If you know you can, you will. Don't play negative records in your head about yourself or the situation. It takes you nowhere. Got a negative attitude? Look at what you're thinking about and dwelling on. Negative thinking creates negative attitudes.
2. Don't make decisions from the emotions or ego. Decisions based on logic, information, and facts, produce the best results. Do your homework, get as much insight as possible, and decide only when you feel comfortable that you have what you need to make that decision, it's your life.
3. For business decisions, seek knowledgeable counsel from trustworthy advisors. Surround yourself with business advisors you know have your back. Well-meaning friends and family are often not the people to discuss business decisions with as their opinions can be biased. Don't trust the decisions you need to make to others. The buck always stops with you.
4. Trust your gut. We all have an intuitive knowing to which we should instinctively listen. Some call it common sense, which is learned over time. It's like anything in life; once it's mastered, you don't think about it as much. It's second nature. Develop your listening skills!
5. Own your decision. If it goes south, don't blame others. Learn from it and move on.
6. Do not worry about what others think about you? Your life is your own, and their opinion really does not matter to your success in life. We live in a society today that markets to people's insecurities and fears (exacerbated by online and social platforms), and companies feed on that fear. When we become

consumed with other's opinions, it puts the focus in the wrong place.
7. Don't bury challenges, problems, concerns, issues – deal with them as they won't go away and will only get worse. The sooner you deal with them, the quicker they will go away. One of my favorite sayings is, "it always seems impossible until it's done."
8. Indecision is a decision. Don't let fear control any decision, especially fear of failure.
9. Never feel sorry for yourself, it leads to a victim mentality.
10. Keep it simple. The bigger the decision, the more stress it can bring in making the decision. Keeping it simple will prevent stress and indecision (paralysis). If it turns out to be an incorrect decision, get up, brush yourself off, learn from it, and move on.
11. Never let the past dictate your future. We know this to be true: Yesterday is gone, today is all we have, and our past does not have to dictate the future. It's imperative to learn from the past, but it does not mean the past will be your future unless you keep making the same choices. **The decision you make today is your future.**
12. Success in life and business is available to everyone, but it's up to each of us to decide what kind of life we want to live.
13. It's up to you. No one else can decide for you. As hard as that may be, it's the truth. I have always loved Nike's "Just do it" marketing. So simple, yet this is where the majority of us fail. We don't just do it. We think about it, but the success in anything is in the doing, not the thinking.
14. Pray about it and commit it to God. Doing this is the most important thing I do in my decision-making process.

No matter your past or wherever you are in life at this moment in time, the right decision can make all the difference in the world. It is never too late. I often told my children growing up, make good choices…why, because I love them and wanted them to have the best life.

I hope that you will take even one thing from reading this and apply it to your life. You're worth it!

PATTY TAULBEE, CEO OF PLANTLIFE NATURAL BODY CARE

Who is Patty Taulbee?

After a successful 30 year career in technology, Patty followed her true passion for natural living and began her journey with Plantlife. She discovered natural eating in the '60s, and natural living in the '70s. Plantlife has been part of that natural progression!

Patty's most important life accomplishment is her family and faith

Tell us about Plantlife

At Plantlife, our focus is on manufacturing the cleanest, plant-based body care products on the market. Since 1994, we've used "old world" formulas combined with the timeless sciences of herbology and aromatherapy. Those two things are the perfect blend of science and nature! A wise proverb says to "choose life that you may live!" At Plantlife, we adhere to that principle in everything we do. Our product's ingredients are derived from the life-giving properties of plants (thus the name Plantlife). We believe that what nature has provided cannot be equaled or duplicated by human-made chemicals and synthetic counterfeits. We have remained dedicated to manufacturing products that contribute to life, health, and are Earth-friendly! Our founding mission statement still holds true today, "For People and Planet."

Plantlife Natural Body Care is based in San Clemente, CA. Plantlife's products are made in the USA and are sold worldwide.

CONTACT PATTY TAULBEE

Email: ptaulbee@plantlife.net
Phone Number: (949) 315-7979
Website: www.plantlife.net
Facebook: www.facebook.com/Plantlife
LinkedIn: www.linkedin.com/in/plantlife

CAPITALIZING ON YOUR TALENTS - BECOMING A CREATIVE ENTREPRENEUR

With BONNI SHEVIN-SANDY, CEO OF DIVERSITY PROMOS LLC

We are all about diversity and inclusion.

Today, almost everyone aspires to be creative from politicians and businesswomen to professional athletes and students. In business, it can be said that being creative, or having a high level of creativity, has become the ace in the hole for competitive advantage in crowded markets.

Defining creativity can be as elusive as searching for the needle in a haystack. For example, when a thermometer is dropped and its housing breaks, the mercury that is encapsulated will separate into small balls. It is frustrating and almost impossible to collect all the balls. It takes considerable effort, given mercury causes continued division, so that every attempt to capture them only adds to the count.

"Creator," "creation," "creativity" are some of the most overused words and ultimately the most misleading ones. Stripped of any particular significance by a generation of bureaucrats, public servants, managers and politicians, the word "creator" became almost unusable.

With the condition to respect the rules of entrepreneurial initiatives, beautiful and successful businesses can be set up in any sector of these industries. They include: advertising, architecture, arts and antique markets, crafts, design, designer fashion, interactive leisure software (electronic games), music, performing arts, publishing, software and computer services, television and radio, film and video,

What is Creativity?

Creativity is the skill that transforms an average worker into the one every employer wants to have on their team. It is the process that brings something from nothing, and what business doesn't need that?

Implementing creativity at work can make the difference between keeping and losing your job, being chosen or passed over for a promotion, and whether you enjoy or hate your hours on the clock.

Creativity is the freedom to love life, excel in your work and sustain meaningful relationships that stand the test of time.

1. All you have is your process.

The key is to build creative thinking into your everyday life by continually asking questions like, "What do I do next?" "Is there a way I could do this better?" "What am I doing that doesn't need this much energy?" "How can I combine steps to create a better product or less time-consuming process?"

When you were a child, you automatically thought creatively. Life and society may have desensitized you to your creative self. As you understand the value of added creativity, you will be surprised how many "great ideas" you start having, seemingly out of nowhere.

2. Commit to creative improvement.

Creative thinking is an ongoing process that requires commitment. Most of us rarely think of it at all, and if we do have a great idea, we rule it out as too weird, too hard or too scary to pursue. Creative geniuses choose to pursue their ideas - at least long enough to mentally play with them and do a bit of research. Like the Nike staff motto, "Be a sponge," and their company slogan, "Just do it," culture-changers are committed to maximizing good ideas.

3. Each field is interconnected with every other field and they influence each other.

This is where the magic happens! As you allow your mind to play with the cross-connections between fields, you find yourself creating shortcuts, modifications and increased value where none had been seen before.

Types of Creativity

The term creativity is used quite often around us, especially lately. This is due to the fact that the need for creativity has become increasingly significant at regional, national and international levels. Basically creativity is everywhere and nowhere, and one often hears and talks about: individual creativity, organizational creativity, and municipal/local creativity.

Individual creativity comes from a deliberate, self-aware process, observing and responding to more "subselves." These "subselves" are internalized, semi-independent components of one's personality that can operate cohesively or conflictually. This process can link different thinking styles together.

Organizational creativity refers to making links between individuals and organizations in a network or system of creation.

In both cases, the key to creativity is the ability to manage complexity and contradiction.

Creative Entrepreneurship

Entrepreneurship in creative industries, and information related to the development of entrepreneurial skills in these industries, are not well known, or rather not fully known. The term "creative entrepreneurship" has become one that refers to the business activity of entrepreneurs belonging to the creative industries.

According to Wikipedia, creative entrepreneurship is the practice of setting up a business or self-employment in one of the creative industries. Creative industry entrepreneurship represents a new way of thinking, a new attitude, which is to seek opportunities in cultural organizations in terms of their cultural mission as a starting point.

A creative entrepreneur is someone who uses their creative or intellectual knowledge and skills to earn a living usually in a business or as a freelancer. This differs from traditional entrepreneurship that has mainly focused on manufacturing and industrial products.

Creative businesses are more active than other types of businesses in promoting innovation. Those who dare to engage in a creative entrepreneurship must face one primary challenge which is the need to find a balance between the artistic side, the financing, and the business development side.

From the term of entrepreneurship in the creative industries (creative/cultural entrepreneurship) derives the term of entrepreneur in the creative industries (creative entrepreneur). This term deals with the realization of a strategy, organizational design, and leadership in a cultural context. This notion characterizes that talented and successful entrepreneurs can turn their ideas into products or services to society.

An important issue that a creative entrepreneur must cope with is the distinct challenge to build and support a business only from creative activities. They must also face challenges normally only small businesses face, such finding an adequate market for their type of creative business. To determine this market, requires asking more from their business objective. By finding their market, the creative entrepreneur can attract capable people, identify financial and technical resources, think and develop strategies on how to compete, collaborate, and specialize to adjust to market changes.

The fact that creative businesses are often developed in special environments characterized by rapid social, technological changes, tough competitions and ephemeral relationships with customers, has already been demonstrated. For this reason, we believe that creative entrepreneurs from some sectors of the creative industries need a business manager or a stakeholder to learn the skills required to lead to the business development, especially in an unstable economic environment.

Creative Entrepreneurs' Characteristics

If you're not already one of us, you may be dreaming of the life you'll have when you finally become an entrepreneur. But first, you need to consider if you have what it takes to make your great idea a viable business.

The following characteristics are features indicative of a creative entrepreneur:

- An entrepreneur adheres to rules and principles only when they add value to the organization and have a potential to attract more customers.

- A entrepreneur experiments with his/her ideas as the first step. The second step is learning from the experience, and the third step is implementation of what he/she as learned.

- An entrepreneur is less afraid to lose and is always keen to experiment in new ventures.

- The entrepreneur is not afraid of creativity and believes that creative ideas will only help their enterprise.

- A creative thinker will take inspiration from new ideas in every area directly or indirectly related to the enterprise.

- A entrepreneur is not afraid to go beyond the industry and enter new markets. This opens a wide range of opportunities to formulate new niches.

- Every product and service is not good enough and has room for improvement. An entrepreneur realizes this very well.

- A creative thinker is interested in bringing totally opposite things together to create new products or services.

- A entrepreneur creates new products for existing services and new services for existing products.

- Creative ideas come more quickly when someone is not afraid to appreciate new ideas irrespective of who comes up with them.

- An entrepreneur shares an idea and is open to feedback that improves and refines the idea.

- Creativity comes from learning different things, whether they are related to the industry or not.

These indicators show that entrepreneurship and creativity go hand in hand with each other. Entrepreneurs are more flexible and seek improvement more than they seek perfection.

Why is Creativity so Crucial for Entrepreneurs?

A thorough observation of the entrepreneurial process shows that creative thinking is the must have "skill" of a entrepreneur for the creation of new ideas. Creativity allows a person to devise interesting processes, which gives so many advantages to entrepreneurs.

But what exactly makes creativity so crucial and important in an entrepreneur's work life?

Creativity leads to success by:

Creating new ideas for competitive advantage. The whole process of entrepreneurship is rooted in creation and exploration of new ideas. When an entrepreneur can generate a new idea that is feasible as well as efficient, it gives them an edge over the competition. The ability to explore different niches is just like a learned skill or a resource that is possessed by an individual.

Thinking of novel ways to develop your product and improve the business. Creativity helps develop new ways of improving an existing product or service and optimizing a business. There is always room for improvement in the deliverables of an enterprise. It is the creative entrepreneur who can assess how to do it.

Thinking the unthinkable. Creativity requires imagination to produce the most obscure ideas. Imagination is needed to cross the boundary of "usual" and "normal" or to think outside the box. This allows entrepreneurs to think beyond the traditional solutions, come up with something new, interesting, versatile, and yet has success potential.

Finding similar patterns in different areas. Sometimes, due to following a routine or a habit, the thinking process also goes along the line of those established processes. Creativity enables people to connect dissimilar and unrelated subjects and make successful entrepreneurial ideas. Merging different fields creates interesting intersections that creates new niches. Most people are afraid of bringing different disciplines together, but the most interesting ideas come from combining different fields.

Developing new niches through creativity and entrepreneurship. In entrepreneurship, it is important that new aspects of traditional business are explored. This can be in the form of changing the method of manufacturing the product, delivering the service, or how they are supplied to the user. All these areas can create a niche that has great potential in business.

Tips for Capitalizing on your Strength

People have made critical investments that had major impacts on their business and financial lives. Surely, the people who invested in Facebook years ago are sitting pretty now. But, the stock markets won't tell you that the best investment you can make is in yourself and your strengths. How do you identify and capitalize on your strengths?

- A good way to identify your strengths is to think about how you solve problems. If you solve problems by collaborating with others, your strengths might include teamwork. Or, if you find you offer a new way of thinking to a complicated situation, creative problem solving is probably a strength of yours.

- Another way of identifying your strengths is to recognize what you most enjoy and identify how you are solving problem or need. Whatever method suits you best is probably an asset of yours. Pay attention to what you enjoy doing most and you will probably stumble across something at which you are genuinely great at doing.

- So once you know your strengths, you can capitalize on them by selling those strengths in a way that is beneficial to your job and your career.

- If you're in the middle of a job hunt, applying for jobs where you can put your strengths to good use is an obvious way to capitalize on your strengths.

- Within the workplace, the best way to capitalize on your strengths is to use them. When a problem arises, put your skills to work. Suggest methods of problem-solving that you can contribute to.

Knowing yourself and your strongest skills can be hugely helpful to your endeavors. When you know what you uniquely bring to the table, you can confidently approach problems in (and out of) the workplace. Capitalizing on your strengths will help you run your business even better, as well as enjoy it more.

Entrepreneurship could simply be the solution for the economic problems of today's world, to bring the most innovative and exciting ideas to reality in ways that solve problems, which is very rewarding on several levels. However, it is a process that can be made even more successful with creative thinking. The above discussion helps us realize the importance of creativity in the entrepreneurial process. Creativity and entrepreneurship go hand in hand with each other. Hence, to be a successful entrepreneur, creative thinking should be consciously done to bring forward the most viable ideas that will sell to a niche or two or more.

Get Started as a Creative Entrepreneur

- If you've decided you'd like to turn your intellectual and creative assets into income, here's how to get started:

- Figure out what you can offer. Make a list of things you know, love, and do, such as doodling, singing, playing an instrument, etc. Remember, your idea doesn't need to be artistic to be considered creative. It just needs to tap into your knowledge base or skill set.

- Determine how your knowledge or skill can make money. Can you create something to sell? Can you freelance your talent? Can you teach or inform people about it, i.e., blogging, informational products, online course, etc? You may have an idea that has several ways to make money, and down the road, it might be a good idea to develop several incomes around your idea. But starting out, choose one, and focus on that until it's up and running.

- Research your idea to make sure there is a market for what you have to offer. Is it something consumers will want? Can you make it profitable? Underwater basket weaving may be your passion, but if there's no one who wants to buy underwater baskets or learn about underwater basket weaving, it's not going to be a viable business. In market research, you want to discover if there are people who are ready, willing, and able to buy, as well as determine who these people are (demographics, wants, needs, interests, etc.) Note, that even if you're starting a blog and offering your ideas for free, to make money, people will need to click on ads or affiliate offers, which means they need to want and be able to buy stuff.

- Write a business plan. If your idea is viable, it's time to start planning and implementing your business. That starts with a business plan that outlines what your business will offer, what is unique about your business, how your business will benefit clients/customers, what you'll charge, your current and forecasted financial situation, your target market and more.

- Decide on a business name. Depending on your business, you might use your given name or you can create a business name that describes what you offer.

- Create your business structure. Many beginning creative entrepreneurs start out as a sole proprietorship, which is fast and easy. However, if you stick with your business, you should consider forming an LLC, which isn't that hard or expensive and offers some protection if you get sued.

- Get a business license. Check with your city or county government office about required licenses or permits. You should also check the zoning department to make sure it's okay that you work from home.

- Protect your creative assets. If you're creating something, consider protecting your intellectual property from thieves. There are three types of protection depending on what you create: 1) Patent for inventions, designs or formulas, 2) Copyright for created works such as writing and art, and 3) Trademark usually for a name, logo or tagline.

- Set up your distribution system. In your business plan, you should have outlined how you're going to deliver your products or services. If you make digital planners, will you sell them on Etsy or on your own website? If you're freelancing your services, will you market them through freelance sites, or through your own website? Whatever you decide, now is the time to set it up.

- Market your business. Once you've got everything in place, it's time to let your market know about it. Marketing is one place many creative entrepreneurs struggle, and yet, your creativity and ingenuity can be an asset. The key things to remember in marketing are:

1) Who is your target market?

2) Where can they be found (what do they read online, what sites do they visit, where do they congregate online and off, etc.)? and

3) How can you put your information in front of them so that they'll want to know more about you (articles, ads, videos, social media, etc.)?

We define Creative Entrepreneurs as follows:

- Somebody working in the creative sector who is able to demonstrate business success in the classic terms of business growth, such as profit, market share, employees. Also, in terms of his or her reputation, their creativity, quality and aesthetic strengths are known amongst their peers.

- Somebody working in the creative sector who has developed a successful social or not-for-profit enterprise in this sector in terms of impact and reach.

- Somebody working in the creative sector who has shown leadership in the industry by championing its development in their country.

- Somebody working in the creative sector who has developed initiatives, such as exhibitions, trade fairs, festivals, or other outlets that develop and grow the market for this sector in their country.

Fact About Bonni Shevin-Sandy

Bonni Shevin-Sandy is the President/CEO of Diversitypromos.com and President/CEO of DARD Design, companies focused on diversity and inclusion. Bonni is also the past CEO at Dard Products, Inc., and. With her entrepreneurial skills and a passion for the industry, she has propelled the growth of both companies. Bonni's passion is helping other entrepreneurs organically grow by helping them through the WBENC certification process. Bonni has a tier one, tier two WBENC, cost savings, global solution. Bonni noted Diversitypromos is a Veteran, military run, and owned certified company. "We give back 10% of all profits to the charity of your choice via our website."

Bonni has invented hundreds of items, and patented over 52 items with an additional 8 patent applications pending, She is proactively exhibiting in Hong Kong twice a year, with an average of 4-5 trips to China per year. Bonni opened an office in Hong Knong, run and managed by an ex procurement global leader who formerly put together the global buying office for NOVARTIS pharmaceuticals in Singapore. Bonni proudly stated "We helped NOVARTIS Global Procurement utilize a cost savings ERP system for global purchasing as well as significant cost savings through the group buy portion of the portal. "When the Hong Kong warehousing and distribution programs became necessary for international business's growth, thats when we hired Michael."

Bonni participates on seven major boards including PRAG (Public Resources Advisory Group), PPAI (Promotional Product Association International) Product Safety, PPAI Editorial Board, ASI Editorial Board and QCA (Quality Certification Alliance). Bonni was presented Entrepreneur of the Year in 2004. In 2005, DARD Design International won an Incentive Marketing Award and from then on has been included on ASI's Multi-Million Roundtable. In 2008, Bonni made Counselor Magazine's Power 50 List, and was named Counselor Magazine's International Person of the Year in 2009. She also made the magazine's 2009 Hot List as "The Innovator" which made her the third woman to be on this list in over 40 years.

With DARD as a founding and accredited member of QCA, Bonni has and continues to be an industry pioneer in product safety and compliance, educating and speaking to other distributors and suppliers within her industry worldwide.

Bonni's patented products are purchased in large quantities as Private products for Sharper Image, Brookstone, Sky Mall. Bonni specializes in gift with purchases, for Shick, Unilever, and P&G. Bonni won her 8th product design award at the International Hong Kong Fair, Ken Fair, and PPAI fair from 2010-2016. Bonni currently has three more items patent pending, said to be her best, most creative, and functional items yet! These items will be ready October 2020.

How Bonni became a Creative Entrepernuer

We asked Bonni how she became a Creative Entrepernuer and her reply was, "I built my name with hard work and dedication. After I established multi-million dollar accounts from start to finish, I took it to the next level by collaborating Distributor/Supplier alliances. I took the partnership to direct end-user presentations, where the Distributor worked on the day to day relationship, and I would present as a strategic partner that did the oversea's manufacturing, factory and social compliance, and product safety. We did a presentation for existing item programs, make it seamless for the end-user, and tied in the creativity that the distributor and myself worked together in product ideation and creative designs that fit the end user's brand and marketing message. In many case's, we gave them what they asked for, but mostly told them what they needed"

Contact Bonni Shevin-Sandy

Website URL: Diversitypromos.com
Cell: 224-628-0386

LAUREN SUSTEK

BUILDING THE DREAM TEAM: IS IT REALLY POSSIBLE?

With LAUREN SUSTEK, PRESIDENT OF BARTKOWSKI LIFE SAFETY, CORP

When you hear the term *Dream Team*, what do you think of?

For a few of us, those words conjure up thoughts of the 1980's comedy starring Michael Keaton (which, as a child of the 80s, I have always loved.) For the majority of folks out there, however, whenever someone says the words 'Dream Team,' their minds drum up memories of the 1992 US Olympic Men's Basketball Team: Michael Jordan, Scottie Pippen, Larry Bird, Magic Johnson – the list goes on. The thought of so much greatness in one place at the same time working together towards a common goal is nothing short of amazing.

This group is known as the greatest sports team ever assembled, and may very well be one of the greatest teams ever assembled, period. Why is this? Each member of this team was an expert in their area, a true artisan of their specific niche within the craft of the game of basketball. Each was a master of his position and brought that particular individual skillset to the team. Each member was then inserted into a situation (the Olympic Games) in which they all needed to come together for the achievement of an ultimate common goal and purpose: winning the gold medal.

A fascinating fact about this whole situation is that the members of this 'Dream Team' only practiced together for six days before the games started.

Six days, 2 hours per day. That's it! It didn't matter, though, since each player understood his responsibility and what he needed to bring to the team for the entire machine to run.

156

Similarly, what good will you be to your organization if you are a jack-of-all-trades and a master of none? As a business owner, it may be more appealing just to lock yourself in your office and crank through projects alone because no one can do it as quickly, as efficiently, or just plain as good as you, right?

Hey, I totally get it – believe me – but I can tell you without question that by operating from and adhering to this way of thinking, you are going to miss the growth of your company.

Now, once you 'get your mind right' regarding this simple truth, the question then becomes: how do you build your own dream team? Just as the initial question sprang from your mind, so too will the solution. You are the one who's going to step into the reality of building a team capable of all the successes you wish for your organization, but how?

Where do you start?

1. Communicate the Company vision

Does your team know what your company does and why it exists?

Can they articulate why your products or services are unique or are a better value over your competition?

Does each team member understand why their role is essential and vital to the organization?

If the answer to each of these questions isn't a solid 'yes,' then you have some work to do.

Your company is only going to be as strong as the people within it, and this strength will come from knowledge. The knowledge is going to come from you.

Now, this does not mean that you are supposed to be an expert at everything or know how to make all of the possibilities for your business a reality; it simply means that you need to share your knowledge about your company with your team.

Share the history of how and why your company started. Educate each team member on the processes that you have in place, so there are comprehension and cohesion among the team as to *why* things are done, and not just *how* things are done. For example, I love when I am training a team member and see the excitement in his or her reaction when a level of understanding of a process is reached that was not previously there. It is as if the light bulb goes off, and there is the 'ah-ha' moment.

When my team learns *why* they are doing this or that, we are then able to take it to the next level and talk about not only my vision but their vision for how the process can be refined or even wholly reworked. All of this is made possible because I have shared my vision with my team, and it grows into *our* vision, which we can then take together to the next set of challenges to help us reach the next level in growth and success. It's that simple, yet also that profound.

As a business owner, share your vision with your team. Once you have shared your vision with them, ask your staff to share theirs. Do career visioning with every new employee after their probationary period; if a new hire at my company has made it past this period, they are going to be fully integrated into our team. I want to know directly from them where they envision themselves in one year, three years, five years, and so on. You can then see if this is going to mesh with your vision and if employment is going to be mutually beneficial.

2. Be clear on Responsibilities and Milestones

My sister, Mary Ellen Derman, is a successful Real Estate Broker and owner of a construction material supply company, so it is safe to say we have entrepreneurship in our blood. We spend a lot of time together, bouncing ideas back and forth and sharing what works and what does not in our respective companies.

Recently I was talking with Mary about our training program and how I was not happy with its effectiveness. We were having a hard time pinpointing what new hires were supposed to be working on at a given time and coming up with reasonable milestones for when complete turnover of duties could happen. Mary asked me, *"Lauren, do you do*

30-60-90's?" My answer was a simple no, and that I was not familiar with that term.

She went on to explain that the first 90 days of employment needed to be broken down into three 30-day increments. All responsibilities are detailed on the plan and divided into one of the 30-day sections. The new hire is given the plan, which has a list of training to be done and skills that need to be learned during their first 30 days of employment. To 'graduate' and move on to their next 30-day employment segment, the benchmarks laid out the need to be met. The first 30-day plan is reviewed every two weeks to ensure the trainee is on track and to address any questions he or she may have. Once the first 30 days are up, a formal meeting is set to review the plan and whether or not the goals were met:

- If the established benchmarks are met, we will move on to the next phase of training and learning.
- If said benchmarks are not met, a discussion is merited to discuss shortfalls as well as goals established to correct this deficiency. In addition, we will meet more regularly to ensure the gaps are addressed while the new training and benchmarks are being worked on.

I can tell you without hesitation that this process has changed the way my company trains and retains new hires. Having a clear picture of the first 90 days of employment is invaluable to spelling out all the expectations and milestones that need to be met and having regularly scheduled check-ins. There is no more guessing as to whether we are on track with training, and there is also much less time spent 'holding on' too long to a poor employment fit.

In the past, I would prolong the inevitable when someone may not be working out. Now we can point back to clear expectations that were written down and agreed to on Day 1 as a basis for either continued employment with the company or the cutting of the company's losses. We are no longer operating in such a grey area, which now saves the company time and resources.

3. Surround yourself with people who are better than you

This is definitely an oldie but a goodie, and there's good reason this idea is still around: because it's true!

The only way you will succeed as the leader of an organization is if you hire people who are superior in areas that you are deficient. Pareto's Principle, or the 80/20 rule, states that for many events, roughly 80% of the effects come from 20% of the causes. As the Leader, 80% of my results should come from 20% of my efforts. It is my responsibility to focus on my 'big rocks,' as my sister would call them, and delegate everything else. I must really hunker down and figure out my strengths, which are my stabilizing big rocks. Then focus on building on those and delegating the rest to those in my organization whose own 'big rocks' are areas I may be lacking.

For example, one of my big rock strengths lies in my ability and skill for organizing people and planning. This is a responsibility that I own. I am also very strong in bringing our services into existing facilities; I developed the process that we use as well as the on-line data system where we document all of our work. These are my strengths. Although I enjoy aspects of accounting and project managing, there is no way that I can do this as effectively as some of the other Bartkowski team members. Therefore, I have taken a high-level attitude towards these tasks: I review specific accounting reports weekly and others monthly. There are thresholds that I need to sign off on prior to large purchases being made. I review weekly productions on projects, all billings, and dive deep into projects every month. Beyond that level, I delegate the responsibility to the team member whose expertise lies in that area.

This process allows me to keep my eye on things while at the same time, it will enable the individuals that are stronger at the day-to-day tasks that make up our accounting and project management departments to shine.

4. Make uncomfortable situations comfortable

In Pat Lencioni's *5 Dysfunctions of a Team,* one of the dysfunctions is the Fear of Conflict. A disturbing trend in today's society is that any type of disagreement is seen as a confrontation and many times is misinterpreted as a personal attack. We see this everywhere: in public, on social media, on the news...and don't even get me started on politics.

Think, I mean, really think about this for a second: someone can be one of our most revered and trusted advisors, say one thing we disagree with, and the next thing you know, they are worse than the gum stuck on the bottom of the soles of our shoes. Why is that? I think it is because we, as a society, have been conditioned to dislike conflict so much that we altogether remove ourselves from situations that are perceived as confrontational. Herein lies the rub: for a team to work, you *have to be able to have healthy conflict and uncomfortable conversations.* As the leader, you can pave the way for the rest of your team by merely asking the questions that everyone else is afraid to ask:

- *Why did we fail to finish a project on time?*
- *Why did we fail to stay within budget?*
- *What went wrong with the disgruntled customer?*
- *Why?*

Now let me just say that I am the Queen of asking 'WHY,' to the point where the rest of the team asks me to move on at times. The reason here is twofold, one obvious and one a bit more layered and subtle.

First, my brain must compute what happened, why it happened, and what we are doing to prevent it from happening again. I will beat a dead horse until it is resuscitated, gets up, and rides off into the sunset! Mistakes are going to happen. I accept this, and I also do not expect the same error to be made more than once. The only way to ensure this is to address what happened correctly. I dig in, and I ask "why" to get to the bottom of things. This is the obvious reason for asking why.

On a deeper and more subconscious level, I also do this so that everyone else in the room sees that it is ok to ask, 'Why?' My employees can see and hopefully understand that any questions asked are not a personal attack. It's not about them or the team being critiqued by pointing fingers or placing blame. It is done to make the company stronger and ultimately better by developing and putting failsafe procedures in place.

When I am not in the room, everyone else will then feel comfortable asking 'why' as many times as they need. I have seen it happen all too often when the leader of the team is not around; everyone avoids questioning the obvious.

Allowing a previously uncomfortable situation to become comfortable and then eventually commonplace in your organization will open the door for trust. And once that door is opened, your team with work together like never before.

5. Allow your staff to hold each other accountable

Piggybacking on the previous topic of making uncomfortable situations comfortable, once that is mastered within your organization, you and your team can focus on accountability.

It will do your business no good if you, as the owner, are always playing the role of 'bad cop.' What do I mean by this? I say it all the time, "Lauren Sustek cannot be the only person policing this office." Let me give you an example applicable to any business to illustrate this point:

In my office, we file all of our contracts in green folders. Why green? First, by using green colored folders solely for our contracts, it easily triggers the brain that the contents are financially related as green is the color of money. Second, when we see a green folder, we know that extremely important and confidential documents are inside and are not items that are to be out just laying around for any reason. This is a well-known rule in our office: *contract folders get put away when they are done being used.*

So…if anyone in the office sees a green folder lying around on someone's desk or in a pile that looks like it has cobwebs starting to form on it, guess what? They are going to speak up and say something! This makes sure that the work is getting done and the clients are getting serviced. Every member of our team has autonomy in his or her position. Now, at a surface level, this may seem like a silly example, but it is clarifying my point that even something as simple as a green folder can be used to illustrate accountability. Everyone within my organization not only learns the rules that we play by, but they are all responsible for holding each other accountable since I, as the leader, simply cannot be everywhere at once.

Whether it is in small or seemingly trivial matters, which as business owners, we know nothing is trivial, like making sure files are put away correctly. It includes making sure the office is well organized and for more important things like making sure proper life safety designs are installed. Also, verifying that we are hitting the project schedules and staying on budget. Each person on our team is collectively responsible for it all, and if they see someone not pulling their weight or giving proper credence to the situation, they have enough trust in the process that they can say something and know that I am behind them.

We have made healthy conflict comfortable and difficult conversations easier to have, and now we have rolled that into everyone on the team holding each other accountable.

6. It's not about the "Buy-In," it's about *Ownership*!

This is a BIG ONE for me.

'Buy-in' is a popular phrase that I have heard in countless leadership training sessions. I'm told that to get my employees on board with the direction the company is moving, or with new market sectors that we are chasing, they need to buy-in first.

Here is the thing though with the whole buy-in philosophy: *What happens after you have it?*

In my experience, most often nothing! Yep, I said it.

So, what if you have buy-in if your team does not take ownership of their responsibilities, their failures, and ultimately their successes?

Giving my employees ownership over their position is the best thing that I have done to nurture the growth of my organization. Being completely honest, I have found that autonomy scares people. Often, the individuals that do not fit in well with the team are those that do not want ownership of their position. They want to be told exactly what to do, when to do it and how to do it. This may be a product of previous jobs and experiences that have ruined an individual's abilities to think for him/herself and to problem solve. It is much easier for people to take direction from others because it provides them with total exoneration if anything goes wrong, born out of the mediocrity-driven mindset, that if you don't take ownership, you can't take the blame either.

Do not get caught up in this insanity, or else you will be micro-managing your team every day of your life. You will have a team that has 'bought in' to your vision yet at the same time will ask YOU to make the call on every decision coming out of your office:

- 20# or 24# paper?
- Single or double-ply toilet paper?
- 10 pack or 12 pack of ballpoint pens?

You get the picture.

Cultivate self-thinking within your organization. I will provide an outline and the end goal that is expected for a position. Think of it like bullet points, or those old Cliffs Notes versions of classic literature we all used to try to get our hands on before the big exam back in high school. This can be a bit rough and will require you to leap in faith. As the leader, I want the person in each role to learn how to get from point A to E without me having to provide them with B, C or D. Once again, allow me to give a very remedial example of what I am talking about:

Our reception position is tasked with cleaning the office 1x per week. When this task was assigned, I did not say, "*Alright, I want you to start in the break room and clean the counter and then vacuum; next move on to the offices where I would like you to wipe down the phones, and desks, etc.*" I simply laid out the expectation (the office is to be cleaned) and the frequency (1x per week). It was up to the person assigned this task to take ownership of it and make it her own. She might have said she 'bought in' to the idea and the importance of a clean office, but without her taking **ownership** of the task, the buy-in meant nothing.

Better still, the lady assigned this task actually came up with a system that was lightyears better than me detailing out how to achieve the end goal! That's not buying in, that is flat out OWNERSHIP of one's role – and that is precisely what I look for.

7. Hire passionate candidates

I was told early on in my career to hire for enthusiasm, not for experience.

I can train someone to do the job. What I can't teach someone to do is be enthusiastic about their job. Now obviously, I'm not suggesting that all conventional wisdom gets tossed out the window: if the position requires a specific skill set, degree, or area of certification, then, of course, we are going to look at that. At the same time, we will also be gauging the candidate's demeanor, energy, and how they are carrying themselves.

Do they have a 'can-do attitude,' or are they offering all the reasons in the world that the past 10 positions in 2 years have not worked out while providing reason after reason why it is everyone else's fault but their own? Once an interview starts going down this road, I already know that this individual is not going to be a good fit for my organization, and, conversely, my organization will not be a good fit for them.

We are passionate about what we do at Bartkowski, and we love bringing on new team members that share our passion. And it doesn't necessarily have to be a passion for our industry (at least not at the beginning), but they do need to have passion in general.

Trust me, you can't train someone to have PASSION, and if you find someone with it, hold on to them. They will contribute their energy to your business in ways you have never imagined.

8. Attitude

Simply put, toxic people with negative attitudes spoil not only the environment but also the morale of your entire organization. Even the most straightforward things become more laborious when the environment becomes toxic. Why is this? Because with folks like this, so much energy is focused on the negative that everything else gets pushed aside or forgotten.

Insist on a positive attitude from your team. This must be a non-negotiable and not just a positive attitude selectively applied to a segment of a population you deal with, but with everyone in every aspect, phase, or chain of operation for your business.

For instance, you cannot have a team member that treats your customers like gold and your vendors like dirt. Your employees have to understand that professionalism with everyone that they come in contact with is vital, as they are an extension of your business and ultimately YOU. I set up our earliest accounts with our vendors. I remember sitting with some of them when I didn't have much in terms of assets and only had a few jobs on my books, but these vendors trusted me and my word. They extended me a reasonable credit line and payment terms. I could not have delivered to my very first customers if I didn't have vendors that were willing to work with me. Do not let anyone sour the relationships that you worked hard to build and nurture. You cannot improve your team cohesion by staying out of the matter. Stay in contact with your team and let them know that following the chain of command is important. And at the same time, if they are ever up against a tough situation and don't feel like they are getting anywhere, remind them that your door is always open. This goes for your vendors and your clients, too.

9. Grow with your team

Life is so unpredictable! You can (and often will) fall or rise several times in a matter of seconds, minutes, hours, or months.

How do you keep your motivation and desire to succeed high? The best way to keep your employees motivated to succeed is to *spend time with them*.

That's it! That's the secret sauce.

Teach your team how to view the company through your eyes. Teach them how to read key metric reports, how you read them (for my company it is production reports, job cost detail reports, P&L's, Balance Sheets, Payroll Distribution Reports and Budget Variance Reports). Do not hide these reports from your team in fear of them seeing how bad or good the company is doing. This is small-time thinking. You are training these individuals to replace you, right? I mean, that's the whole idea, isn't it? If that be the case, which it is, how can they replace you if you are not teaching them what you do, and how you do it!

Another essential piece to this puzzle is to stay in communication with your employees and ask them their opinions often. It may be tempting to make quick, snap decisions on your own, but the goal is to groom your team into taking big decisions on themselves. Take the time to train your employees. Share with them your experiences, downfalls, successes, and map out all resources, milestones, delivery dates. This will pay dividends to your organization.

Invest your time in growing your team, and you will learn and become more than you ever imagined.

10. Your team transcends your business

The majority of this chapter has focused on your professional team, but always remember that your team does not end there. There is an entirely separate team that makes your success possible, and that is your personal team. This can be your spouse, parents, siblings, and friends. There isn't one successful person I know who does not attribute at least a part of his or her professional success to their personal team.

I have had people say to me, *"I don't know how you do it all with your business, your involvement in organizations, raising your children..."* and I just laugh. Why? Because I know that by myself and on my own,

I'm lucky to get out the door every morning in one piece. But with the support of my personal team behind me, I am unstoppable! Do you have a personal team? If not, you need to build one.

Work is something that we do; it is not who we are. As business owners, for us, that line gets even more blurred. It is so easy to get lost in the search for worth and validation through the attainment of professional achievements, ranks, and titles that we forget our most famous 'titles' are usually the ones we have outside of work hours. At work, I am Lauren Sustek, President of Bartkowski Life Safety, but outside of work, I am Lauren, the daughter that gave my parents a run for their money growing up (and we can all luckily laugh about it today.) I am Lauren, the sister and the friend that will defend you with everything I am. I am Lauren, the wife, and mother who provides for my family and knows that they are more valuable to me than anything else on this Earth.

Don't get too wrapped up in building the professional network that you forget about your personal team. If you do, you risk losing yourself, that is, who you *really* are.

Who is Lauren Sustek?

Lauren Sustek is president at Bartkowski Life Safety Corp. She founded Bartkowski Life Safety in 2010 after working with a General Contractor for several years prior. She brought a new vision to the life safety industry that focused on customer-tailored solutions. Lauren has assembled a team of like-minded individuals, and together they have grown Bartkowski into an industry leader

Conversation with Lauren Sustek, President of Bartkowski Life Safety, Corp

Tell us more about Bartkowski Life Safety, Corp

Lauren: Bartkowski is a specialty contractor that focuses on providing life safety services to both new and existing facilities. In new construction, we provide essential life safety measures such as fire stops, smoke sealants, and perimeter containment. In existing facilities, we ensure that clients' buildings stay compliant as both the code and the buildings change. We provide barrier surveys and code corrective remediation, damper inspections, and fire door inspections and repairs. Bartkowski is a certified Women Business Enterprise (WBE) and Disadvantaged Business Enterprise (DBE). We have worked in 24 states and pride ourselves on the consistency of our operations, no matter where our work is being performed.

Who is your client base or focus audience?

Lauren: Our clients are a mix of Facility Managers, General Contractors, Subcontractors, and Government Agencies. Although our client base is very broad, the common thread is each of these customers' unwavering commitment to life safety. Each client understands the importance of the services that we provide. They know that when they hire Bartkowski, they will not have to question if we have done our job correctly.

Tell us about your competition and how do you different.

Lauren: When a client hires Bartkowski, they know that they will end up within compliance. Our approach to a project is unlike any company in our space. We are often brought in during the design phase and become an integral part of the project team from the beginning. This allows for a seamless flow from design into the execution of the project. We recognize that there is an outlay of our resources upfront without knowing if a project might come to fruition, but we do not let the uncertainty discourage us. We treat every project and every client with the same degree of service. This level of both detail and commitment to every phase of a project is how we differ.

What does success look like to you?

Lauren: Success, to me, is peaceful. When the days, weeks, months, and years end, and I look back and ask myself, *"Have I experienced more happiness, smiles, and love than I have stress, frustrations, and worry?"* When I can answer yes to this, there is a profound sense of peace that exists, and I know that I am successful.

What is an issue or problem within your industry?

Lauren: As crazy as it sounds, people do not take life safety seriously. You might be reading this and say to yourself, *"There's no way that this is possible!"* Well, I'm here to tell you that it happens more often than I would like to admit. Some of it is blatant, and some of it comes from a lack of education about what passive fire protection is. That's why it's our mission at Bartkowski to educate everyone that we come in contact with about the importance and the need for a comprehensive life safety program to which they should adhere.

What are the barriers you are facing in your own business, and how did you overcome them?

Lauren: One of the barriers is being a woman in the construction industry. This barrier is a constant work in progress. The more I support other women in construction, the easier it is for us as a collective to continue to chip away at this decades-old wall.

Another barrier has been my age. I started my company at a relatively young age, and there have been several times that I have been asked my age point-blank as if the individual was better able to gauge my competency based on the number I shared! Yes, it's outrageous. I was able to overcome these doubts through education and becoming more involved with my trade-specific associations. Through further training and certifications, I honed my skills in life safety. By becoming more involved in associations, I was able to assemble a network of individuals that knew more than me, so when I am faced with a question I don't know the answer to, I can confidently say, *"You know what, I don't know, but I know where to find out."* This has really helped squash the notions that I am too young to be at the helm of the ship.

The final barrier is being a mother of three small children while growing my business. I am always trying to juggle the personal and professional aspects of my life. This is a work-in-progress as well, since both my personal and professional life change so quickly and so often. What helps me is talking about it. The more I open up to those around me about my uncertainties and insecurities on being a mother and a business owner, the more I discover that so many women have the same struggles. And as crazy as it sounds, when you know you are not walking the road alone, the road itself does not seem as rough.

Through the growth of your business, share with me maybe an obstacle or barrier you faced and how you overcame it.

Lauren: In my prior answer, I spoke of my age as a drawback. As I have grown my business, I have become more determined to make sure all of us at Bartkowski are considered the 'go-to' when tough situations or questions come up. We support continuing education for all employees. As long as we are a reliable resource for our customers, my age and my company's age will not matter.

Where do you see your business in 3 to 5 years from now?

Lauren: In five years, I see my company continuing our growth trajectory and opening satellite office locations. This will help us service the client base that we have gained outside of our home market. We will still have a core focus on life safety with a more significant concentration on providing our services in existing facilities. This remediation division will be our next big push.

What are you doing to work towards reaching those previously shared goals?

Lauren: We are continuing to recruit talent that will allow us to grow and expand. During our strategic planning sessions, we have open discussions as a group about what the company has accomplished and what our new goals and benchmarks are. I am personally pursuing existing facilities that require our services to build a base of clientele in this division.

As a certified Women-owned business, why would you recommend to other women in business to become certified?

Lauren: The apparent reason is to help a project reach its WBE goals. When you are being considered for a project, and when all things look equal, sometimes that little bit extra that you can bring to the table through WBE certification is enough to push you over the top.

The less obvious answer is that women should become WBE certified because of the network that comes along with it. The women's groups that I have joined because they were, one way or the other, WBE focused, have been invaluable to me. My network is full of professional women in my industry that I can go to with questions and for advice. And in turn, I can provide my experiences and knowledge to others. It is incredible how much easier things get when you don't have to fail 1,000 times before you get it right because you now have a network of women that will tell you their lessons learned. You can bypass so many missteps! Get certified and start growing your network.

Contact Lauren Sustek

Email - lauren@bartlsc.com
Phone Number - (708) 498-0004
LinkedIn - www.linkedin.com/company/bartkowski-life-safety-corp./
LinkedIn - https://www.linkedin.com/in/lauren-sustek-b90828b/

ACHIEVE SUCCESS AS A MOM-PRENEUR

With JULIET AYDIN MALKI, WIFE, MOTHER AND CEO OF JEWELS OBSESSION, LLC

"You can juggle motherhood while running a business and be great at both."

Being a mother as well as an entrepreneur is a strenuous task, but as George H. Brimhall said, "If you avoid difficult things, great things will avoid you." So even though it is challenging, passion for work can make anything possible.

For any woman in this world, motherhood is a beautiful feeling. Looking at the face of a child is a sight of delight and contentment for a mother. There is a unique bond between a mother and a child. While on the other hand, a zeal for work turns the mother into an entrepreneur, striking a work-life balance is profound to be a successful mompreneur. One has to stick to a particular role at a time. There should be no room for remorse or regret while being either a mother or an entrepreneur. Both the positions should be equally enjoyed and performed with sheer grit and determination. One should take pleasure in parenting as well as entrepreneurship

Raising a child is not a cakewalk. It requires efforts from everyone around you for him/her to grow and learn different things. Whether it is your spouse, friends, or relatives, all of them contribute towards the progress of your child. A child who learns from many people around him/her has a more dynamic personality.

Being a stay at home, Mom is a privilege and a gift. For which in the world where bills are unavoidable; Mom entrepreneurs face numerous challenges. They put in twice the efforts to what other entrepreneurs give. This duty of them demands multitasking and strong will. To make things work your way and to maintain balance in your personal and professional life, you'll have to remain patient and balanced.

Here are the top 7 STRIVES to finding a balance as a mom entrepreneur.

Strive #1 ~ Funding

Most moms rely on their savings or their credit cards to start their business. Many moms do not seek for investors to help get their businesses off the ground, mainly because we moms have subscribed to the false honors badge of being a supermom who can do it all alone, without asking for help.

Unfortunately, statistics show that when moms do pitch investors to raise funds, it is a proven fact that women, especially when they are moms, have a harder time securing venture capital funding than the opposite sex.

Strive #2 ~ Motherhood Responsibility. No excuses!

As Moms, it is our responsibility to prevent the guilt card from starting a new business; otherwise, guilt will cause them to give up on their business or potential success. Unfortunately, Mommy guilt is something all moms experience.

Let your children be your reason, not your excuse.

Strive #3 ~ Find your luster

It's not a secret for anyone that one significant flaw we share as women are, we downplay our worth, we undervalue our efforts, and we do not own our achievements.

We do not like to be perceived as arrogant or "full of ourselves," and God forbid someone thinks we are bragging – sure, we can brag about our kids, but not about ourselves.

Stop focusing on your shortcomings and let your light shine. Yes, the gender wage gap is real, but you may be underpaid because you don't let others know how qualified you are, you don't give yourself the credit you deserve, and you don't charge what you are worth. You can still be humble on the outside and confident on the inside!

Strive# 4 ~ Self-care

As Mothers and entrepreneurs, we are pulled in every direction, and we often fail to add ourselves to our list of priorities. We want to do it all – for everyone! We push ourselves too hard; we overextend ourselves, failing to say no to what does not serve us or failing to say yes to what will grow us.

Strive #5 ~ Look for Support

It is widespread not to have a proper support system in place to help those Mom entrepreneurs being successful.

Be sure to find a mentor to provide guidance, inspiration, perspective. Find access to tools and connections, and provide yourself with a healthy dose of reality, as needed. Juliet has had some incredible women in her life as leading examples and as a support system to keep pushing forward.

Strive #6 ~ Being respected in your field

Often as moms, we are seen as less productive, more distracted, and less ambitious than the opposite sex. Women and mom entrepreneurs are sometimes forced to prove ourselves before someone will take us seriously and give us a chance. When faced with aggressive opinions, learn to use them as stepping stones to move forward.

Strive #7 ~ Always stay true to yourself, no matter the setbacks.

You do not need to act or think like a man or be compared to other women. You do not need to be more of this or less of that. Being a mom helps you be a better entrepreneur, and your voice, your gifts, your skills, your abilities, and even your demeanor are instrumental to your success in any industry. Do not be afraid to be your true self. If we all have our gifts, be willing to present your authentic self. Those who find its value will appreciate you, and for the ones who don't, that's okay.

Here are a few tips to secure success as a mompreneur:

- Commitment and Plan: There are several businesses in the market, but not each of them is successful. Plan to make your business stand out so that it can reach out to the right people.

- Flexibility: The plan that you make should be flexible. You should be able to make changes when required. Even at the eleventh hour, you should be able to adapt to the necessary changes.

- Finances: You should watch your finances. Some businesses need a little investment, while others require a significant investment amount. According to your business, plan how much and where would you invest.

- New Opportunity: Today's consumers are always on a lookout for something better. Seize a new opportunity that can help your business to excel. For a caterpillar to become a butterfly, it has to come out of a cocoon.

- Time Management: A significant part of a business is to manage time. Both your family and business need your attention.

When a mother entrepreneur runs a business, she tries to juggle between two different worlds. It is essential to offer the best to both worlds. When spending time with your child, your heart and soul should be there and vice versa for business.

Who is Juliet Aydin?

Juliet Aydin Malki is known as a creative jewelry designer. She is the CEO of Jewels Obsession, LLC, and also the owner and Brand creator of Guliette Verona. She started her love for jewelry when she was a little girl, spending her childhood in her father's jewelry store in Germany. The establishment of Jewels Obsession, LLC, has become one of the leading online jewelry distributors opening the door for her famous Guliette Verona Original Crown Ring. With her hard work and never-ending efforts, the original Crown Ring has successfully become the number one seller in Women's jewelry on Amazon!

Juliet firmly holds the Jewelry industry near and dear to her. Having grown in the Fine Jewelry retail industry, it has helped her to communicate and meet some incredibly knowledgeable people throughout the years.

Professionally, Juliet has a tremendous appreciation for the time and efforts that are put into the design and labor process of creating jewelry. Whether it's a client who creates from their vision through the CAD Design Process; or merely purchasing a sentimental jewelry stock piece, it is undeniable that fine jewelry has always been passed down from generation to generation. The value and genuineness of it all are utterly fascinating and irreplaceable. She believes the art of jewelry is forever purchased through love, and when love is involved, you cannot go wrong. She recently became a member of The Women's Business Enterprise National Council as they are always doing updates and modifications towards their marketplaces to help customers with successful order fulfillment.

Juliet Aydin Malki aims to bring awareness to the hardworking American Jewelry manufacturers and American designer brands in the United States of America.

The jewelry design industry is extensive; therefore, she hopes to be available for other fine jewelers and manufacturers to thrive in the online market and avoid massive product listing fees. Through vigorous technology growth, Juliet believes marketplace expansion for particular subject fields is a dire need. She hopes to excel in these modern updates during an era where people have a difficult time making decisions when faced with too many options.

Juliet believes these efforts will help small business jewelry manufacturers get more mainstream and thrive in the online world.

Conversation with *Juliet Aydin, CEO of Jewels Obsession, LLC*

Jewelry has always been a part of society. Tell us something about your venture, which deals in jewelry and accomplishments you've made.

Juliet: I have been around the Fine Jewelry Industry all my life. Having worked in three fine jewelry stores and taking the leap of venturing out on my own, I expanded my world of jewelry. I became the CEO of Jewels Obsession, LLC, and Designer for Guliette Verona Original Crown Rings.

The establishment of Jewels Obsession, LLC, has become one of the leading online Jewelry distributors opening the door for our popular Guliette Verona Original Crown Ring. The Original Crown Ring has successfully become the number one seller in Women's Jewelry on Amazon!

Due to its high demand, we have been welcomed by Walmart, and the sky is the limit! We hope to reach all Women and Queens leading the way!

The most significant accomplishment has been my three beautiful children, who continue to inspire me daily.

Who is your ideal client base?

Juliet: Great question. Our client base is both male and female. In an ambitious world, it is paramount for a male counterpart to support women, particularly for those women in business. I have been fortunate to have a partner who supports my efforts of expansion in my field.

Having years of experience in the Fine Jewelry Industry, we recognize that men love buying sentimental jewelry for their loved ones, and women luxuriate into treating themselves. Trust and integrity have always been our priority with our clients as well as our manufacturers.

We strongly believe that serving clients takes you from success to significance.

In this world of competition where everyone wants to stay on the top, how do you manage to stand out?

Juliet: Competition is a natural part of any industry. Being a parent of two daughters, The Original Crown Ring differs because I stand by my product and its representation of what it means to me.

Competition, although difficult, is a healthy way to grow and better client experience.

Being a Certified Business through WBENC, would you recommend fellow Mompreneurs to become certified, and why?

Juliet: Being a certified Women-owned business will give you the opportunity and appreciation to be among a beautiful group of women. Their strength is silent, but it seeps through just by being in their presence. They do not feed intimidation; they bring forth knowledge, power, and courage to move forward in your industry. Therefore, I would encourage female entrepreneurs to take a leap and get certified through the WBENC. Thank you, WBENC, for making my industry heard and being an advocate for all women!

If I was searching to purchase a piece of jewelry, what advice would you share with a consumer?

Juliet: If I were to share advice with a consumer, I would like them to comprehend that fine jewelry is that moment of reflection where you are amongst your life and your accomplishments. It is a sentimental work of art that is precious because it can be passed from generations on end. Jewelry came to denote human connection and commitment.

In Mediterranean ancient times, jewelry was offered to the gods and was used to dress up statues. Dating back to 3000 BC, The Royal Tombs in ancient Sumner, a discovery was found of the most fabulous collection of all times. There they found mummies encrusted with every imaginable type of jewelry worn. The ancient Egyptians also formulated jewelry as sacred. They firmly believed that gemstone colors such as Emerald, Rubies, or Turquoise reflect aspects of our personalities. Gold was particularly associated with the sun and was always used in crowns and ornaments for the pharaoh and his priests. This tradition is still used in religious forums today.

This is why we have such an appreciation for fine jewelry. The crafting and labor process of jewelry is particularly magnificent. I have witnessed first-hand; it is an impeccable work of art that is not only marveled at but also worn. I believe that in genuine gemstones, in particular, they hold profound properties to its wearer, where its symbolization is a reflection of its owners, such as finding a unique piece that matches your birthstone or religious beliefs. Jewelry is personal and sacred. Whether it is given as a gift to symbolize your love; or purchasing something special for yourself, the best part is that it doesn't end there. If you decide to buy an fantastic diamond ring, even though designs may change and modernize throughout the years, you may always take the diamond out of its setting and input it into any other design you wish to create.

The possibilities are endless with jewelry. It should never be overlooked as a piece of clothing, handbag, nor alongside fashion jewelry that can be worn for a short while, but rather its incredible ability to have a part of someone's heart held onto for generations.

In a world where online shopping has been the number one form of product purchasing, I recommend finding yourself a personal jeweler. They can assist you and your whole family for anniversaries, graduations, engagements, or any other important milestones in your life.

Thus, I encourage consumers to seek personal jewelers and acknowledge their appreciation rather than associate jewelry alongside standard accessories.

Growing up in the Fine Jewelry industry and meeting clients who understand the value of Fine Jewelry has been a profound experience to appreciate that it is found under the earth's rough terrain. Fine jewelry is enough to hold its own; it should not be alongside categories with belts, sunglasses, shoes, or handbags.

Having experienced the difficulty in locating a valued jeweler, we have dedicated ourselves to providing consumers access to the Fine Jewelry Industry to be introduced in the first online Fine Jewelry Marketplace.

Now online consumers will have access to this exceptional spectrum with leading personal jewelers, manufacturers, and reputable jewelry brands.

Contact Juliet Aydin

Contact: Email: jewels@jewelsobsession.com
Website URLs:
1. http://www.gulietteverona.com
2. www.JewelsObsession.com

Phone Number: (818) 279-1450

IT TAKES A VILLAGE

With PAMELA STAMBAUGH, PRESIDENT AND FOUNDER OF ACCOUNTABILITY PAYS INC., BEHAVIORAL CHANGE MASTER

"The entrepreneurial journey starts with jumping off a cliff and assembling an airplane on the way down." Reid Hoffman, Founder of LinkedIn and PayPal

" I love entrepreneurs – it takes much heart to be one. The joy of entrepreneurship far outweighs the fear and the courage it takes to be on the roller coaster ride." Pamela Stambaugh, President, Founder of Accountability Pays

Everyone experiences fear in their lives. And, as part of their journey, every successful entrepreneur has had to face and overcome their fears. People who have a dream, know they have an idea but are too risk-averse to fulfill that dream. They stay in a position they often don't like and later look back with regret.

Fear can take many forms such as being afraid to change, being afraid of failure, and being afraid of what others think. Fear often disguises itself as excuses, for instance, 'I'm not ready to start my own business because I don't have time, I'll do it later.' Underneath this excuse is fear.

Below are three Drivers of human behavior that will break through the fear of becoming an entrepreneur.

The Vision Driver - Following Your Bliss

Having a Vision of how you want to live your life is a powerful driver. Creating a vision starts with realizing a future view for yourself because you want to make a difference in the world and for others. Focusing on your passion or desire to be fully self-expressed will be a big part of your courage and motivation to take the leap into entrepreneurship. Maybe you want to cure cancer or reverse the damage being done by humankind to our planet. As an example, MADD, Mothers against Drunk Drivers, was started by a mother who lost her child because of a drunk driver. Perhaps you love sky diving, so you want to teach this skill to others. Maybe you are an artist, that is your true expression and your gift, so you create and sell your art, which begets your business.

A clear and well-defined personal vision will make you unstoppable in realizing your passion and bliss.

The Belief Driver – Overcoming Naysayers

Having a strong Belief is the passport to achieving your vision. You can have a vision for the future, but if you don't really believe it in your heart of hearts, you won't be a successful entrepreneur.

To really believe in something means that you will be unrelenting and unyielding in pursuing your vision no matter what struggles you face, or who tells you it can't be done. Fred Smith, who started FedEx based upon his college thesis, was told by his professor that his idea would be a failure. Fred believed strongly in his vision and pursued it. We _all_ know how that story turned out!

A strong belief will not get rid of your fear, but it will allow you to face fear, and, as time passes, your fear of becoming an entrepreneur will give way to fulfilling your vision.

The Action Driver – Take The First Step And Don't Look Back

The third driver is Action. Feel the fear, and just do it! Follow the Nike motto, "Just Do It."

If you haven't developed a vision and belief system, you will eventually realize that you lack the touchstone that drives your commitment and energy for your passion. When your mindset is clear and firm, then it's time to jump onto the pathway of becoming an entrepreneur.

Once you take your first step and action in your business, your fear will seem less ominous. You will feel energized and enthusiastic about your vision and. When fear returns, you've got the idea, belief, and actions to counter the unease of risk and potential failure.

In sum, to power your entrepreneurial adventure:

1. Create a **Vision** of your passion and bliss
2. Have the **Belief** that you can achieve it
3. Take **Action** to get started

Where do you find yourself today?

How do you know if you have fear of starting a business? Here are some symptoms.

1. You have a vision and a contribution you want to make. However, you are not moving forward with a dream. Also, you always had a negative perception about business and your leadership ability.
2. You are trapped in old beliefs about taking risks and being able to make a difference.
3. You lack self-confidence in carrying out your business activities and think you have to make the journey alone.
4. You hate selling and marketing and do not understand financial matters.

Steps To Move From Fear To Self-Confidence

1. **Protect yourself from naysayers.** If you have people in your life who don't believe that you can do achieve your dream, shield yourself from their influence. Guard yourself from naysayers, even the news. While you are building the muscle of moving from fear to trusting yourself, any negativity has the potential to bring you down, so don't let others' concerns limit yourself.
2. **Stay in a place of positive expectation**! It is essential to positively expect great results no matter what you see in front of you, therefore, stay in faith that what you want is on its way

to you. An often-used powerful affirmation by successful entrepreneurs believes it is already here, even though you have not manifested your realization.

3. **Repeating it, TAKE ACTION. Then take another action, and another.** Once you are able to shield yourself from the negativity and stay positive, you'll want to continually be taking action. You can't just sit there and say, "Ommmm - bring it to me." It's not going to happen. **As my father used to say, "God helps those that help themselves."** You've got to be in action in your plan. **On those fatiguing and challenging days, my mother would say, "The difference between hope and despair is a good night's sleep!"**

I Dare You – Do You Have The Guts?

As a woman entrepreneur, you will face many obstacles. Overcoming these obstacles includes being self-expressed, learning, growing, expanding who you know yourself to be, and that is exhilarating. With these inner experiences come inner peace and true self-improvement that leads to being the full contribution you know yourself to be.

When knowing yourself as reliable, Courage will be present. You will venture into courageous action, persevere, and withstand nearly any fear, or difficulty. Synonymous with Courage are terms such as mettle, spirit, resolution, tenacity, and the mental or moral strength to resist opposition, danger, or hardship. Courage implies firmness of mind and will strengthen you in the face of danger or extreme difficulty.

Of course, you will feel fear, but if you are afraid of the consequences of making a mistake, Courage teaches you to learn to accept consequences of bad decisions gracefully, seeing them as learning moments, not failures.

Like the airplane that leaves San Diego bound for New York, initially, the plane's path is varied and not straight until it eventually hones in on its target. This aptly describes the entrepreneurial journey as well. When you don't know what you don't know, you will vary widely from your straight and narrow path to desired results. As you begin to predict the future based on your experiences from the past, learning from your mistakes, your way will straighten. You will learn what your customers want, and how much they are willing to pay for what they want, and you adjust accordingly.

How Does a Woman Entrepreneur Build Courage?

Fear is a lurking, potential saboteur. It can be debilitating and can limit your ability to experience life fully. When faced with opportunities to give up and yield to the obstacles you will indeed face, some internal – like fear, and some external – like competition or naysayers, you need to buck up by reaching out for help, by taking a break and looking with fresh eyes. By knowing it's OK and this, too, shall pass.

Sometimes fear is smart and obvious. If a bus is heading in your path, clearly you should swerve to avoid it. Your fear is appropriately alerting you to danger.

But if it's not "smart fear" truly protecting you and it doesn't forward your vision, CHOOSE not to give it expression. Distinguish between useful fear and limiting fear by taking time to learn the origination of your fear. Perhaps your fear is lack of confidence to tackle the task or fear of failure.

Some ways to develop confidence are:

- promote excellence in your area of expertise
- invest in your vision, mission and strategic plans
- surround yourselves with empowered, like-minded coaches or mentors
- align your business with programs and services to stand out from your competition

Where is your focus? Focus on building faith and becoming faith-full. Faith is the opposite of fear. The objective is not to put all of our focus on eliminating fear, but embracing lifeskills that allow you to freely move forward. It has previously been stated that fear is **F**alse **E**vidence **A**ppearing **R**eal.

You may think you're lucky if Entrepreneurship isn't scary for you, but fearlessness isn't the antidote, fearlessness is a psychosis. If you're not just a little bit frightened, you're either not taking risks, or you're blind to them. Either that or you just don't care enough. Paul Allen and Bill Gates have reported that they always had some level of fear every day at Microsoft, even years after it was the world leader in computers.

"It's ridiculous to say we'll conquer our fears that we're going to wake up one day and not be afraid. I've done hundreds of public presentations before audiences from 10 to hundreds, and I still have that little knot in my stomach before I speak. We've got to recognize fears for what they are and manage them." Pamela Stambaugh

A healthy level of fear is often helpful to perform at our peak ability. The fear that holds people back is rooted in a lack of self-esteem, and leaders are no exception to that condition. Pamela noted, "We all walk around carrying baggage. For some, it's a lightweight; for others, it's cumbersome. Much of this baggage contains question marks over whether we're 'good enough' or whether we can make it."

Advice on How To Build Courage And Fight Fear From A "Behavior Change Master."

1. Be Accountable and Authentic; Ignore your Inner Perfectionist

One trait entrepreneur's share is the ability to set goals and be intentional about the outcome of the business. Pamela admits that her first and only goal was to woo a client — and she did. Her first client was a renowned professional speaker, and thus her primary target market became professional speakers. She was an independent contractor supporting The Ken Blanchard Companies' international expansion, training their international partners in marketing their programs. She organized their international conferences in Europe and Malaysia. She wrote the marketing plans for their expansion into Canada and Mexico, including analysis of the competitive landscape. Shortly after that, she co-authored a book called Market Smarter, Not Harder.

Pamela's story resembles that airplane path mentioned earlier – in the beginning, very approximate and not very intentional. Her entrepreneurship emerged out of a lifestyle goal, not an entrepreneurial goal. She was very fortunate that her passion led her to today. Her main strengths were her willingness and ability to fail and the ability to pivot.

Conversely, the intentional entrepreneur starts by naming and claiming an overall company mission and builds upon intentional smaller, achievable tasks that serve as steppingstones. Those small goals and actions will make the company mission more digestible and less intimidating. Entrepreneurs are often type "A" perfectionists, but everything does not have to be perfect to start testing versions of your product or service. Start building your website and talking about your business to anyone who will listen.

Setting realistic goals is especially important when you're starting your business as a side hustle while working for someone else. "Getting started is tough in part because you're making a change in your daily routine. In my case, I didn't have that job security," Pamela observed, "but I had financial security." For many who would like to be their boss, how do you go from side hustle to leaving your J-O-B and taking the leap of faith?

2. Don't Go It Alone, and Learn to Pivot

Over 30 years ago, Pamela Stambaugh started her business with a bundle of fear and the desire to have a "Lifestyle Business" where she could make her unique contribution to leadership effectiveness. In the early days of her entrepreneurial adventure, being home-based was not cool – today, it is much more prevalent. As time progressed and after many years of the flexibility that the lifestyle business afforded, Pamela learned, "It Takes a Village."

That "Village" or "Tribe" is any group of people — an association, a peer group, a regularly convening community where give and take occurs, within which you can be authentic and feel safe to ask for and receive experienced, helpful counsel. Today, Pamela has several villages. Some she participates in for a fee with experts and peers, and others are comprised of seasoned professional friends with a common purpose. Consider that as an entrepreneur, you will want to grow both personally and professionally!

Pamela acknowledges two particularly important villages, like Vistage, that helped her grow into the professional she is. She said, "Right here in this book, I want to acknowledge Marianne Ellis, Janet Lienhard, and the CEO Success Community for being a village which I appreciate and in which I grow. I also want to acknowledge Mark LeBlanc, Growing Your Business, a favorite coach of mine for many years whose wisdom rings in my ears every day! His tribe is my tribe, too!"

Additionally, Pamela learned to PIVOT — to not just keep doing what you're doing expecting a different result. THAT is the sign of insanity! She learned not to get buried in minutia, but to seek the long view, then look at the short picture, then return to the long view. Make choices, be willing to fail, and when it's time, PIVOT. Pamela is excellent at the pivot — there's juicy and encouraging news for you in her story.

In 1999, she was trained in the Harrison Assessments Talent Solutions™, adding this capability to her leadership development solution set, enabling her to bring people solutions. Pamela's business had begun as a marketing and sales consultancy. Several years later, she became trained in Systems Thinking by two masters, Bill Schwarz and the late Stephen G. Haynes, thus adding strategic planning to her consultancy. Pamela was speaking and training on many continents at that time. When the towers came down in New York, and the Pentagon was struck on 9/11, she was in Washington, DC. She experienced first-hand the horror of those airstrikes. Those were lonely times, frightening emotionally, and physically.

After 9/11, she felt the urge to stay closer to home in San Diego, at which time she became a Vistage chair coaching CEOs and their executives, a position she occupied for five years in addition to her consultancy in strategic planning. Within Vistage, she added executive coaching to her broadening capabilities. It was here that Pamela came to value her "Village" of fellow Vistage Chairs with whom she met every month and on whom she came to rely as voices of reason and collaboration.

Then there was the day post-Vistage and while coaching, providing team building and support for human resources as well as senior executive teams — about thirty years into the business — Pamela said something new. She said, "I want a successor. I want what I've built to survive my contribution." She wanted her business to become *"A Legacy Business."* It was a new kind of excitement, the opportunity to transfer her knowledge, skills, abilities, tools, and relationships to build others into winners with her experience.

Excitement AND a new fear emerged for Pamela, only this time that fear was more momentum for action than the limit to productivity. By now, Pamela KNEW it takes a village, and she didn't feel alone.

If you're in your early entrepreneurial years, an excellent question to ask yourself is, "What triggers my fear?" Once you name and claim your fear, how do you overcome it and build a successful business? You find your courage to take the first step, that's what! Then, you wholeheartedly commit to your idea and believe in yourself. Pamela's lesson, "It Takes a Village," is an excellent lesson to learn early on in your journey because no entrepreneur has EVER succeeded alone.

While the ideal would be for the owner to craft a clear picture of what he or she wants the business to look like in the long term, it is perhaps a good first step to decide whether he (or she) will follow the "lifestyle" or "legacy" path. So, what's the difference?

Like Pamela, an owner finds themselves on the "lifestyle" path when personal reasons outweigh business reasons. For Pamela, it was the freedom to travel with her husband and also to have purposeful work at a time when the circumstances of the economy were not supportive of finding a traditional career. For others, it might be to provide a beautiful home or car, vacations, or extra cash for toys like snowmobiles, boats, etc. In lifestyle businesses, most (sometimes all) available money is drawn out of the company as it is made. The business might be used to buy "perks" such as country club memberships and purchase doodads for personal benefit. Or, as a side hustle, the money for perks may not even be relevant. People have their own internal drivers who, like Pamela's, can change over time.

Don't leap to the right/wrong conclusion about lifestyle versus legacy business! There are impacts good and bad to either choice. The long-range implications of a lifestyle business are that when you are ready to exit your business, you may not have anything (or very little) to sell. It doesn't have an asset value. Remove the owner from the company, and there is no business. For Pamela, that's been JUST FINE with her in the past. Pamela is motivated to make a difference. If she's making a leader into a better leader with her coaching or team facilitation, she's having a good day.

The owner desiring to leave a legacy conducts business in a very different manner from the owner of a lifestyle business. For example, the legacy owner is content to defer the payout into the future.

For the past two years, Pamela has been building structures and systems that enable growth beyond her personal capacity so she can leave the business in the care of a successor five years from now. She has trained support staff, so the company is not dependent upon her. If she goes on vacation, like a Timex watch, the business keeps on ticking.

In summary, the two business pathways – lifestyle or legacy – are very different, and both require vision and belief in yourself. Fear will be present. Fear can be corrosive, personally, and professionally if not appropriately managed. Keeping fear in perspective enables pivots, finding your village, and taking actions commensurate with your vision and your belief in yourself.

Who is Pamela Stambaugh?

Behavioral Change Master in Leadership Development

Having been brought up by an Episcopal minister and psychologist in Wyoming, Pamela came by her interest in people and the impact of dynamics between them naturally. Pamela graduated from Lewis and Clark College in Portland, OR, and holds an MBA from the University of San Diego. After 30 years, Pamela is an experienced executive advisor with an established reputation for coaching executives and teams to elevate to their ideal performance. Her father was not encouraging! While in high school, she expressed a desire to follow a business career. Her father's response was, "We'll send you to secretarial school." So rather than begin with a business degree, she earned a bachelor's degree in English Literature Education and taught school for four years before starting her MBA.

Today Pamela provides the executive and team coaching skills plus the CEO Tools by Aprio™ framework, which provides the leadership cadence to align and engage business executives to elevate their performance and results significantly. In the event opportunities would exceed her personal ability to fulfill on them, Pamela can call on back up professionals because she has her village.

Pamela also utilizes the Harrison Assessments Talent Solutions™, which is an appropriate and in-depth assessment to executives, emerging leaders, and professionals on their behavioral preferences and tendencies. Her unique ability to achieve long-term positive behavior change in leaders is recognized by many executives today.

Pamela displays visionary leadership needed for the success of enterprises in today's world, especially important given stiff competition and technological diversification. The unique combination of CEO Tools™ and appropriately utilized assessments plus her wisdom as a coach and facilitator give her bragging rights: **She helps executives and their teams to succeed in what matters most to them.**

Pamela has brought her skills to large well-known companies in a variety of consulting capacities, including GE Healthcare, CA Technologies, CBIZ, Abbott Labs, and Bombardier, among others. She has co-authored two business books and traveled to speak and train around the world. As a Vistage Chair for five years, she first met Kraig Kramers, the originator of CEO Tools and Jim Canfield, author of CEO Tools 2.0™, who at that time was Chief Learning Officer of Vistage and today is Managing Director of CEO Tools by Aprio™.

Besides being President, Founder of Accountability Pays Inc. and a CEO Tools facilitator, she also holds the title Managing Partner of Harrison Assessment Talent Solutions™, an assessment measuring 175 behavioral preferences and tendencies applied to the entire human resources lifecycle of solutions including acquiring, developing, engaging, and leading talent. She has utilized Harrison Assessments™ in her work for 20 years, being one of the early adopters and current leaders.

Pamela's Core Competencies

Pamela, the professional speaker. Being on the platform with Dr. Ken Blanchard, the One Minute Manager, in Atlanta, GA presenting research to the managers of all SKF manufacturing plants from around the world brought me to a new level of performance. That was 25 years ago. I shared the platform with Ken again in Greece for a public audience a year later. Both experiences were frightening AND exhilarating, both offered profound growth for me as a speaker, and I added profound value for these business leaders. **Creating worth for others makes an experience worthwhile for me.**

Pamela, the international trainer. I have trained in three continents. Some experiences stand out; here are two. I trained Coca Cola executives in Greece for a day, all men except one woman who was pregnant, in a room billowing with smoke. Greece had no discernible limits on smoking in public places until 2019 when a law was passed that seems to be finally gaining traction. Somehow, I, and they, got through the experience. To this day, I wonder how the pregnant woman's unborn child fared.

I also trained the leading Turkish beer company's senior executives for a day in Turkey right after their return from a successful fundraiser in the United States. They were pretty full of themselves at that moment. During our day together, they discovered they didn't agree about some basic business assumptions. **It always surprises and delights me when I can uncover the undistinguished, and it makes a difference.**

Pamela, the facilitator. When I was in Europe working with the Blanchard Companies' partners, facilitating their learning one country at a time, I consistently received feedback that I was very effective at facilitating group interactions. Of all my professional competencies, this is my favorite role! I enter the context of the client's making. From this trusted position, I get to bring the attention to what hasn't been said, what hasn't been seen, and what needs to have a light shone upon it, so movement that has been blocked can occur. **I am listening, echoing, reframing, creating space for something to show up that will forward the action, get a better result.**

Pamela, the Vistage Chair, (i.e., CEO peer group facilitator). I would ONLY onboard CEOs who were both open to feedback and willing to take action on their insights. Any peer group process can and should validate that leaders can be available not only to business results but to optimizing the employee experience as well.

My first Vistage member owned a manufacturing company. He was a member during all five years of my Vistage chairing tenure. During that time, he brought on a partner and supported moving the plant to a lower-cost area of the country. He eventually sold the business to that partner, becoming a solopreneur, providing sales support for the organization. He pivoted, freeing himself from an executive role that no longer suited him. His journey demonstrates courage, not unlike my current journey to bring in a successor at this time in my own business. Having helped multiple entrepreneurs, including him, exit their businesses, it will soon be my turn.

Pamela, the consultant's partner. I have many experiences partnering with other consultants; this is one ongoing client relationship of which I'm particularly proud. My husband, Larry, and I share a client, Edge One Medical, a fast-growing medical device company in Chicago serving Fortune 100 Companies. They have grown 400% in the last five years, becoming the leader in their field and quadrupled their staff size as well. During this exceptional growth and success, Accountability Pays has been responsible for supporting executive development and hiring decisions. The standards for hiring and performance have been set high, and the accountability for adherence to the culture and producing results is part of the highly recognized fabric of the company.

And last but not least, Pamela, the executive coach. I'm choosing to let a client speak on my behalf. An Executive Vice President who hired me to coach three of his people said this:

"We hired Pamela Stambaugh to coach three high potential individuals for one year, one of whom manages a team of 5 people, and the other two were still individual contributors with intentions to be given managerial responsibilities. The results were as we had hoped. With the manager, in addition to the Harrison Assessments™, Pamela applied the Leadership Impact Survey™ to pre- and post-test this individual's effectiveness in garnering discretionary effort and employee loyalty. His results in that regard improved measurably, which was consistent with our desired outcome to have him focus more on his team and less on his output."

"The individual contributors also improved in their effectiveness as executive team members of our small division within the larger organization. One coach produced an outcome from a project that lasted over six months that had an impact on the entire industry in addition to a positive revenue and profit impact for the company. The other was able to improve his ramp-up time for new projects and be more effective as a communicator. In both cases, these were the intended and desired outcomes."

"We were quite satisfied with the results Pamela produced as a coach to these individuals. I highly recommend her as a coach and appreciated the additional clarity and depth of perspective provided by the tools she used in her coaching process."

Pamela Outside of Business; the Personal Pamela

Pamela's hobbies include photography, athletic endeavors, writing, and a particular kind of collaging called "Soul Collage™." Some of her best moments have included drinking fine wine with her husband at spectacular locations around the world.

Business and personal merge and meld when you're an entrepreneur. Having resided in San Diego since 1984, Pamela and Larry currently live in a downtown condo in the marina district. She is committed to ensuring the sustainability of San Diego, both economically and environmentally. Her service to the community includes chairing the Distinguished Speaker Series (DSS) at the University Club, and she is a past member of the San Diego Rotary Club. Pamela served a three-year term on the board of the San Diego MIT Enterprise Forum, including a chair. Also, each year, Pamela mentors one MBA student from her MBA Alma Mater, the University of San Diego.

Accountability Pays received the 2019 award for Business Management Consultant in San Diego.

Accountability Pays is a Certified Women-Owned Business. Pamela was selected as Vice-Chair in the San Diego "Forum" for WBEC-West (Women Business Enterprise Council West). She is a founding member of the CEO Success Community, a community of fellow Certified Women-Owned businesses.

Conversation with Pamela Stambaugh,
President and Founder of Accountability Pays Inc.

Pamela, when did you first decide you wanted to become an Entrepreneur and start Accountability Pays?

Pamela: I started as an entrepreneur when I completed my MBA, and there were no jobs. It was an economic recession. At that time, my husband was traveling a lot for work, and I wanted flexibility, so I started my own business to provide myself that flexibility, and it stuck. I fell into my passion.

As we discussed already, many Entrepreneurs have a great deal of fear when they launch their business. Did you have any fear, and if so, can you tell us why?

Pamela: Because I was new to San Diego with a newly minted MBA, I had a great deal of fear but mostly from having to circulate among folks in the business community. However, I also knew I had a successful husband, so the fear wasn't financial; it was social. People are shocked people when I tell them that as I'm a socialized introvert — YOU would never know! I did plenty of teeth-gnashing and crawling back into my shell for many years. Now I program the appropriate balance between "out there" time and "in here" time.

With 30 plus years in business, you overcame those fears! Share your secret with us.

Pamela: I can honestly say I still have my moments because I take many risks that are out of the range of my comfort. I have always taken risks, moved forward, felt the fear, and done it anyway!

Many would concur with me that it is a monumental milestone to have a successful business for 30 plus years. Can you tell us your keys to sustainability?

Pamela: This business has sustained because I have persistence and tenacity and have kept 70% of my clients year over year. Accountability

Pays mainly grown because of referrals. I know that when I communicate to my community — my village — they will listen for the value I can provide THEIR clients, THEIR friends, by making a referral. Likewise, I will do the same for my community; we help one another!

Help us to understand Accountability Pays Inc. and what you do for your clients.

Pamela: First, we meet clients **where they ARE**. They need what they need, but they want what they want. Bringing both to bear takes respect for what they already see they want, and courage to show them what they need and perhaps hadn't yet wanted.

Accountability Pays Inc. provides behavioral change solutions. When they are ready, we provide executives practical tools to communicate, execute, and optimize for success. We can utilize rigorously researched and statistically validated assessment tools for people's alignment. **I continuously remind myself, "Keep it simple so that implementation is tangible, realistic, and moves the needle."**

People are the most valuable asset in an organization; nearly all leaders agree. And they are fundamentally quirky. They may not like their boss – it is well-known people leave people they don't leave organizations! Their values might not align with those of the organization.

These complex and diverse human dynamics issues impact performance and organizational results and are reflected in leading research. For example, a whopping ~71% of employees are not engaged, a reality that has not improved over many years. The cost to organizations is profound –$450 billion to $550 billion a year in the U.S. in lost productivity – and it is addressable!

That 71% level of dissatisfaction can be dealt with directly by a manager and his/her direct reports. Using the Harrison Assessment™ engagement and retention report, we address the leader and employee shared responsibility of engagement, complete with a specific, actionable coaching program. The utilization of CEO Tools™ brings process clarity and significant behavior change.

Notably, due to the shifts in age demographics, a surprising 72% of companies are anticipating imminent leadership turnover, and many companies are not aware of the significant loss of institutional knowledge and leadership skills. As a leader in a sizable organization, the highest skilled, highest paid, hardest to recruit, and hardest to keep people is about 15% of your employees. What we do is extend their lifespan by anywhere from two months to two years against the national average.

We do that by a strategy that encompasses sourcing – a methodology for getting those people who are, by nature, inclined to stay. At the game time, we work on a culture that supports and keeps those particular people engaged because the 3rd largest reason people leave is because of the environment in which they work, that's the culture you've got.

The third thing we do is ensure that the people around them stay because one of the reasons people leave is because other people are going.

We have a system by which all of those things happen, starting with the most valuable people in the organization, that 15 % of key employees.

Many of us would look at Pamela Stambaugh and say you are incredibly successful. You are a Women-Owned Business with 30 plus years in your industry. Share with us what you feel Success is for you.

Pamela: Success has layers including integrity, being a trusted advisor, having the courage to speak to power and being an equal, eyeball to eyeball, standing with, and for that leader whose business I impact.

With a client: I address a leader's BEING not just his/her decisions. Like water, culture runs downhill. Where people dynamics are creating organizational mischief, those issues find their source at the leadership level, executive decisions with unintended consequences. Blind spots. Fear at the leadership level, even personal ego-driven vendettas.

I once conducted a two-day strategic planning retreat where the first day the elephant in the room was evident in the lack of energy and engagement, yet the cause remained undistinguished. In a probing conversation with one team member that evening, I learned that the owner, who was married, was having an affair with someone in the organization.

As my first order of business on day two, I called him out. That was the responsible thing to do, or they would have paid me for nothing! He was stuck and lacked the courage to get himself to a different place. In that room, he resolved with his team to put his integrity back in. Once the elephant was distinguished and dealt with, everyone could be present and focus on their organization's strategic issues. Because inner forces motivate people, a leader must be responsible for who they are BEING not just what they are saying and doing. http://bit.ly/chicken_egg_leadership_recipe

In my business: I have recently taken concrete steps of having a successor in the business, including establishing myself as a Sub Chapter S corporation. I am actively seeking my successor to join the company and grow into the leader of Accountability Pays to continue fulfilling on the mission, that *Leaders Lead with Integrity, with Love, and Listen for Peoples' Greatness — that people, the planet, and profits may thrive!*

Personally: Anticipating the ups and downs and managing them without fear, trusting myself, being present for my husband. Getting a good night's sleep EVERY night! Remembering my morning spiritual practices and keeping myself fit and physically active.

We all have that thing in business that helps us build the foundation. That door opening experience! What was your one thing?

Pamela: It was a direct result of my village. You've seen these people's names before in this chapter. Not only did Bill Schwarz introduce me to Systems Thinking, in 1999, but Bill also introduced me to the Harrison Assessment™. Little did I know that it would become the most robust and effective tool on the market today, bringing predictive analytics to acquire, develop, lead, and engage executive talent. Likewise, Managing Director Jim Canfield, with CEO Tools 2.0, as Chief Learning Officer at Vistage, taught me much of what I know as an executive coach.

As a Business Leader, I know you have faced barriers. Share with us an obstacle or barrier you faced and how you overcame it.

Pamela: After experiencing 9/11 in Washington, DC, I didn't want to travel so much for work. My courage shrunk to staying in San Diego, focusing on coaching senior executives as a Vistage Chair, and simultaneously running my own consulting company. Today as I advance my systems and processes, I bring on additional people and take on more, larger clients intentionally, and with planning, the business grows.

Can you expand more about the Harrison Assessments™?

Pamela: Harrison is a two-way assessment because it measures the degree to which the employer and employee will meet each other's mutual needs and expectations. Consequently, it predicts engagement, retention, and development needs. Moreover, this tool is very useful in team development of my clients to raise trust, unbridled engagement, and "no kidding" accountability.

What are you doing to work towards reaching your 3 to 5-year goals?

Pamela: In a word, planning. With the one-page business plan, the key performance indicators are SO visible, and that makes it clear in tracking our business progress and our own progress as well as keeping track of the results of my actions.

Who would be your ideal client?

Pamela: Two target client groups for different reasons and with different decision-makers.

First, my sweet spot as an executive coach is working directly with senior executive teams in middle-market companies, companies of 1,000 employees, or less that are growing, where I can deliver value directly, and the result is seen immediately.

When working in large organizations where human resources systems already exist, we are sought out to support and train the use of our tools that support their objectives.

Why should they do business with Pamela Stambaugh and Accountability Pays Inc.?

Pamela: We are nimble, accessible, highly trained, and qualified. The Harrison Assessment™ is a global tool referred to as a Unicorn by those seeking worldwide impact from one purchase decision. CEO Tools is vetted with 10,000 success stories.

Most successful leaders recognize that their primary asset walks in and out of the door every day. It's all about the people. We elevate the leadership and their team to the ideal accountability, trust, and culture required for complete success.

Contact Pamela Stambaugh

Phone: 619-231-0195 office
Email: pstambaugh@accountabilitypays.com
Website URL: https://www.accountabilitypays.com/
LinkedIn Link: https://www.linkedin.com/in/accountabilitypays/

JULIE PARMAR

MARKETING YOUR BUSINESS WHILE BUILDING YOUR BRAND

With Julie Parmar CEO of Vegetarian Naturals®

Are you a woman who has decided to venture into business? Do you want to build your brand to grow your business skills? Is it essential to brand your business? What's your digital brand worth? It can be worth a lot. You can measure its impact in reduced marketing costs and increased revenues for your business.

But if you're not executing that brand consistently, branding leads to confusion. You miss opportunities. Customer acquisition costs skyrocket. If you are branding the wrong way, it leads to lost opportunities and expenses.

Brand your business with a digital marketing strategy to increase visibility and engagement across marketing channels. Convert those interactors into customers through effective branding for success.

Let's review the numbers that prove branding is vital to your business and breakdown branding through digital marketing into 9 basic steps.

What is Branding?

Branding is anything that helps your target customers instantly recognize your company. Traditionally, your brand includes things like your:

- Company Name
- Logo
- Color schemes
- Slogans

- Fonts
- Advertising methods
- Message

The more consistent you are with these necessary branding components, the more likely someone is to recognize your brand. A brand isn't who you are as a company, and it's not who you strive to be. It's how people perceive you as a company.

You can be the most honest, high quality, customer-focused company out there. If people don't see you this way, you need to work on your brand.

That's branding 101. Business leaders have long known that branding is the key to success in any industry.

But the Internet blew branding wide open. It gives you the ability to brand your business in ways that customers not only respond to, but they prefer digital branding. It better aligns with how people make buying decisions in a modern age.

But why is branding so important in the first place?

Why You Should Brand Your Business: products and services rarely stand alone.

Why should someone hire your HVAC company to repair their air conditioner this summer? They could employ companies A, B, or C who do the same thing? You may even be competing with company D that offers HVAC repair services.

Customers choose you because of the feeling that you build up around a brand. If your brand is built on honesty, people feel this when they see things that remind them of your brand. This feeling compels buying decisions.

If you don't have a brand, they feel nothing. You might entice them with a one-off discount. People may make occasional impulse buys. But they feel no connection that drives them to schedule an appointment. The only reason they would come back is if you gave them another discount. You can't grow a business like that.

Branding by the Numbers

A Harvard study found that 64% of people name "shared values" as the main reason they follow a brand. They trust that the brand provides them with accurate information and follows through on what they say.

53.9% of people don't trust commercials, infomercials, or ads from a brand they don't know. You can run ads all day, but if people don't trust it, they don't buy it. 78% of people say that they trust companies that build their brand on providing relevant, custom content.

Branding increases company visibility online by over 400%. That translates to more traffic to your physical store. Convert it to sales.

On average, a brand increases revenue by 23%. Digital marketing costs go down as revenues go up when you brand your business.

Do You Already Have a Brand?

It's worth asking. Maybe you already have a brand behind your business. Let's find out.

95% of businesses say they have a branding strategy. But research shows that only about 25% are consistently executing their brand strategy. Only 60% of the content produced by these businesses even attempt to conform to any kind of branding standard.

Nearly half of their marketing efforts are entirely "freestyle." "Let's try this." "Oh, that looks like a good idea." You know the drill.

- Are you having trouble generating the revenues that you expect from your marketing efforts? Do customer acquisition costs make it barely worth your while? Are you getting bad reviews that seem unfair, but happy customers never seem to leave reviews?

- Are your customer retention rates abysmal? Are you continually running deep-discount promotions to get new business?

If you answered yes to any of these questions, then you may have a brand, but you're not executing it effectively or consistently.

71% of people say they feel confused when a brand is inconsistent. That's not a feeling you need to be associated with your brand. Brand your business for success online. Here's how to set up a solid branding foundation with digital marketing.

1. Establish Your Overarching Goals

These are those evergreen goals that don't change. Build your brand strategy around them. Some of the top targets for business branding are:

- Being able to charge a premium for your brand. People will pay $1,000 for the latest iPhone when they could get a comparable Samsung for $400. Why? The brand.

- Retaining customers. Conservatively, loyal customers are worth 10X their first purchase after expenses. You have a 5% chance to sell to a new customer. You have a 20%-30% chance to sell to an existing one.

- Higher conversion rates. When you convert a higher percentage of traffic more efficiently, acquisition costs go down while revenues go up.

If your goals are different, consider what they are as the first step to brand your business for success.

2. Revisit Who Your Customers Are

One of your branding goals is to brand your business in a way that your target customers love. You need to know who they are to do this.

Create buyer personas. These include, among other things, the following about your ideal customers:

Goals

- Challenges
- What they like
- Where they hang out

Use real customer data whenever possible to create these. If you haven't created personas by writing everything out, do this first to brand your business more consistently.

3. Have the Right Website User Experience

Having a responsive website is the single most crucial factor in developing a digital brand. It's the home base for everything you do to brand your business online.

Whether you share content on social media, run ads, or send an email, you direct them back to your website. From there, they'll explore your services, review case studies, sign up for free trials, buy, and more.

If the website is slow, not mobile-friendly, or hard to navigate, this impacts how the person sees your brand. You won't make the sale. They won't come back.

A responsive website is the centerpiece when branding a small business. That goes for an online shop or a brick-and-mortar local service provider.

4. Make Your Site Visible in Search Results

Over 50% of website traffic now comes in through the organic search results of search engines like Google. "Organic" results exclude the ads. Google uses an algorithm to rank websites in the search results.

- The higher your rank, the closer you appear to the top of page

1.

- 92% of organic search clicks happen on page 1. Around 1/3, go to the top spot.

- What does this have to do with branding? The more often people see your brand in various places, the more likely you are to generate interest and earn clicks on your brand.

That's how to create a growth cycle through branding. More people will recognize your brand because you're visible. Your brand becomes more noticeable when Google sees that people like your brand. The cycle continues and expands, and the results are increased revenues.

5. Develop a Written Style Guide

Do you have a written branding style guide you can use as a reference? If not, create one immediately. You need a document to align your digital branding strategies.

On the Internet, it takes 7-13 touches with your company before a person becomes a customer. During these touches, the customer is checking you out. They want to see if you share their values as a business.

If a person doesn't know it's you because you're not following a style guide, you've just missed an opportunity for a touchpoint.

As you brand your business across the Internet on social media platforms, email and beyond, have a clear guide that includes:

Branding 101 (logo, slogans, etc.)

- Font styles

- Font sizes for various headings and body text

- Color palette

- Video/Graphics/Animation Styles

- Language style and terms/How you relate to people through images and words

- Patterns/Backgrounds

- Message/Angle — how you show that you understand their goals and challenges

- Outreach methods/channels

- C.T.A. (Call to Action) and other button styles

Brand your business. As you execute your branding strategies, return to this document. Stick with it. Update it if you determine that something works better. But don't haphazardly stray from it.

6. Listen to Your Customers

One of the top things that people can say about a brand is that they listen. You pay attention to what people are saying about you online. You always work to make things right when something goes wrong.

In addition to comments and reviews, listen through analytical tools. Gain insight through Google Analytics and more advanced paid software.

As you listen to your customers, you'll gain insight into how you can further develop your brand to improve how they perceive you.

7. Create Branded Content

Once you have a style guide, you can begin generating content. This includes any content that you use to:

- Increase brand awareness

- Build trust

- Generate leads

- Nurture leads
- Convert leads into paying customers
- Nurture existing customers
- Increase promoter activity

To meet objectives in these areas, create:

- Social media headlines
- Blogs
- Videos
- Landing pages
- Ads
- And more

No matter what type of content you're creating, it will follow the style guide you've created.

You may find yourself distributing content in places that limit font styles or other branded elements. Compensate by including other style guide elements that help people quickly identify your brand when they see it.

You have your website, content, and style in place. It's time to make your presence known across the Internet to brand your business. That requires engaging people through something marketers call multi-channel marketing.

8. Build Your Brand Digitally with Multi-Channel Marketing

Multi-channel marketing is reaching people through various channels online. You do this for several fundamental and essential reasons:

- The same people who are on Instagram are probably on Facebook, and so on. Some people may prefer a specific channel.

- Some channels are more effective at connecting with people in various stages of the buyer's journey.

- Different channels can better showcase your brand.

- Being in multiple places increases your touchpoints. If it takes up to 13, you'll get there more quickly.

- Being in multiple places makes you "feel like a brand," not just a single social media profile.

Each channel has a unique way of connecting with customers. Channels not only include social media platforms like Facebook; they include email marketing, Ads, display ads on websites, and any other digital channel you choose.

While your branding stays the same, what works well on one channel doesn't always work on another. As you brand your business across channels, it pays to understand how to build a brand on each channel.

9. Leverage Your Brand with Advertising

Now that you've built a brand, it's time to leverage that brand to get the highest return on your paid advertising budget. Because you have a brand that people recognize, people not only know who you are, they feel something when they see your brand.

If you've worked hard to create that "good" feeling through branding, then more people will click and convert.

When using social media ads, make sure they visually align with your presence on the corresponding social media site. When someone sees a display ad on a website, they should instantly recognize you. That's because you're using branding elements consistent with your brand.

Even when you post a text ad on Ads, the language you use should remind people of your brand.

Brand Your Business for Success

To get the most out of your branding efforts, be consistent. Develop a style guide and clear branding strategy. Follow this guide across channels. Increase visibility and evoke positive feelings toward your brand.

Maintain some Consistency

Consistency is the key to the success of any venture. It is not enough to come up with strategies. It pays to craft a timetable against which the plans are to be executed. That is because many projects fail to see the light of the day due to poor execution.

'Consistency' entails maintaining a set pattern of activities and their rollouts. You might have to invoke the assistance of a trained specialist to do this. Many of the strategies in vogue at the moment are way too complicated to handle alone. Patience is also a necessary trait.

Remain True and Loyal to your Brand

Other than crafting your brand, you have to deliver to its promise.

If people do a followup to see if the brand fulfills its promise, they should always find a "true" verification of fulfillment. Otherwise, you have lost a customer because they will never try out another product from your company.

Therefore, it is better to make only realistic promises. The promises you make should be well-anchored in reality with an accurate representation of your products. Be swift to apologize for any disillusionment as that can go a long way in assuaging any anger.

Select appropriate Marketing Avenues

Ultimately, it is whether your products reach the market that counts. You may have wonderful products, but they will not do you any good if you cannot channel the same message to a suitable market or audience to build their trust. That phenomenon calls you to select an appropriate marketing channel.

The channel you opt for has to be relevant to the needs of the people concerned. It should be one that projects your brand in the correct light. To receive the best outcome, the channel should be tried and tested to deliver the best-ever sales and performance responses. Then again, you have to exercise patience and tact to get the best of them.

Carry out Extensive Market Research

Before venturing into marketing your business, you must see to it that you carry out extensive market research. Get to know the expectations of the people who would most likely purchase your product. Study their behaviors, trends, and other patterns that have a role to play.

As you carry out the research, be mindful of the image that your brand is to portray to others. That is because images leave an everlasting and permanent mark. Take this time to impress upon the potential clientele your personal strengths.

Design and Distribute Templates

There are no better tools to expedite your sales and marketing endeavors than the templates. For this reason, we strongly urge you to design and use the templates extensively for your marketing undertakings. These templates also form the standards against which future marketing enterprises are to be based.

As you design the templates, take good care of the color schemes and other decorative aspects of the company. These include the company logo, looks of the templates, the feel thereof, and other unique identifiers. They have to be consistent, fancy and match the company ethos pretty well.

Integrate your Brand

To be assured of the best-ever outcomes, you have to integrate your brand. Integration, in this case, means making every aspect of your operation align with the ethos of your firm and its overall goals. This includes things like how you answer your phone, the kinds of attire your workers wear, and so on.

Such an integrated approach is, by all means, strongly recommended as it boosts your visibility, makes it easier for you to be noticed. And, of course, it's simpler for your audience to remember in the long run. You have to settle for a scheme that is easier to identify and utilize it to the fullest.

Monitor and Review

From time to time, spare some effort to monitor and review your progress. While you are at it, compare your past progress and achievements on the one hand and the expectations you have on the other hand. This may imply the use of many analytical tools, as well.

Some of these may be flow charts, diagrams, trends, and patterns. This procedure is crucial as it is not only complicated but also far-reaching. The data or deductions derived from it may often have profound implications. You may wish to enlist the services of an expert researcher in it.

Nurture your Loyal Customers

Building your brand also entails nurturing your loyal customers. By doing this, it will definitely require you to create a profile and study your clients keenly. Identify those who have the potential to bring in higher sales revenues and narrow down to them. Narrowing to them entails keeping a keen eye on their engagements with you.

Take your time to call, follow up, and even text them from time to time. Then, find out any serious issues they may be going through and address them promptly. To make them even more robust, consider giving them discounts or other forms of preferential treatment.

Set your Goals and Budget

Everything you do has to happen within a particular budget framework. That is why it pays to set and work within a stipulated budget frame. You do not want to spend too much money and time where it is not needed.

You have to carry out an honest assessment of your financial resource endowment as a critical first step. Then, craft a budget against which to operate and adhere to it strictly. Take care that you make any adjustments from time to time to be alive to any new realities that may come along.

Conversation with Julie Parmar, *C.E.O. of Vegetarian Naturals®*

Why create a vitamin? I mean, it is already a very occupied space in today's market, isn't it?

Julie: Actually, believe it or not, one day, I was searching for a vegetarian OMEGA and D.H.A. gummy supplement for my two toddlers and came up empty. I could not find anything! So, since I couldn't find it, I said why not develop my own line.

Nearly every product I found contained gelatin, animal ingredients, and other harsh chemicals, colors, and flavors I did not want to give to my young daughters. Also, being a vegetarian family, I wanted my toddlers to achieve health and wellness through nutrition. A daily supplement was essential to achieve a balanced nutritional program for my picky toddlers.

I knew there was a need for a natural vitamin in the market, and Vegetarian Naturals® was born! I decided to develop my own line with the ingredients and ethics I was looking for to support overall wellness for healthy growth and development. Voila! Vegetarian Naturals® Kid's Whole Life™ OMEGA & D.H.A. Gummies and Kids Whole Life™ Bear Necessities Multivitamin Gummies came into existence.

See, Kids Whole Life™ means supporting your child's total health through all ages and stages. From toddler to teen and everything in between! All of our products are free from artificial sugars, colors, flavors, and high-fructose corn syrup. Our products are manufactured and packaged in an F.D.A. registered and inspected facility that is GMP-certified.

Share your perception of Success?

Julie: Success to me is gaining marketing and advertising presence in the competitive market by educating people on our mission of sustainability, healthy growth, and wellness promotion. I mostly use all forms of social media to accomplish this and build brand awareness in the process.

So, all industries have related issues, what is a problem you see in the Vitamin Industry?

Julie: There are many issues in the vitamin industry. Most importantly, gaps in the manufacturing processes. Vegetarian Naturals® guarantees that our products are Third-Party tested and formulated in the U.S.A. All of our products are manufactured and packaged in an F.D.A. registered and inspected facility that is GMP-certified. However, one barrier that I have encountered in my business is the vast competition. As a small based business just starting, it requires funding to build the right marketing and advertising strategies. Still, through competitive advantage in the marketplace, we've been able to overcome some of these obstacles.

The most impactful barrier we have faced is being a small owned business with limited funding for global marketing and advertising campaigns. One way I have overcome this is by focusing on our internet presence and expanding in that marketplace arena.

What sets Vegetarian Naturals® apart from your competition?

Julie: Vegetarian Naturals® believes in a natural approach to health and wellness, so each product uses natural colors, sugars, and flavor blends to support overall wellness for healthy growth and development. Sustainability is an integral part of the Vegetarian Naturals® philosophy. We are committed to a dietary supplement line that is 100% vegetarian. That means our children's vitamin gummies do not contain gelatin, and we do not test on animals. Exemplifying our mission, we are reducing our carbon footprint in the environment.

There is much competition in the supplement market. To name a few, Smarty Pants, Nordic Naturals, and Hero Nutritionals are a few of our competitors. Most importantly, we pledge that ALL of our products are vegetarian formula, gelatin-free, fish-free, and made with natural sugar, color, and flavor blends. Sustainability is what drives Vegetarian Naturals® mission and defines us as a business.

Contact Julie Parmar

Email: Julieannparmar@gmail.com
Phone No: (5 1 2) 6 2 9 – 8 2 5 4
Facebook Link: https://www.facebook.com/vegetariannaturals
Instagram Link: https://www.instagram.com/vegnaturals/?hl=en
LinkedIn Link: https://www.linkedin.com/in/vegetariannaturals/

PROFESSIONAL FEMALE IN A MAN'S IDUSTRY

With April M. Davis with ADS Design Solutions

"Ginger Rogers did everything Fred Astaire did, she just did in Backwards and in high heels."

This quote highlights the very essence and reality of females in our society.

You rarely see another soul in the lady's room or on the job site. On too many occasions, you've been mistaken for someone's assistant. Sound familiar? For many young, successful women, professionally "making it" means learning to master male-dominated workplaces where boys' clubs still somehow pervade.

Every woman wants to be admired and respected in her industry but is often afraid of being too confident or perceived as being too aggressive in the pursuit of greatness. While you cannot control the opinions people have about you, you can control your actions to get people to take you seriously.

And along the way, April picked up some practical tips for thriving in the male-dominated industry —even when the gender ratio isn't in your favor.

The Squeaky Wheel Gets the Grease

Chances are, your male colleagues are constantly vocalizing which opportunities and projects they want—and you might be sitting there, working hard, and waiting to get what is rightfully yours.

Sadly, most bosses or potential clients are too busy to figure out what the most equitable project allocation is, and it often comes down to who yapped last to them about that hot media deal or the new partnership your company is launching. If you aren't good at grabbing your boss in the hall or during your morning coffee break and bringing up the projects that excite you, then schedule a formal time to check-in at least once a month and let your boss, clients or even potential clients know what been going on.

Don't Be Anyone's Coffee or Lunch Getter/Create Boundaries

Creating boundaries and being wary of the blurred lines between personal and professional relationships is essential in getting people to take you seriously as a young female in your industry. Although it is vital to maintain a pleasant, collegial environment with colleagues and engagement, it is crucial to establish limits around those relationships. Always try to keep it professional.

How many successful men in the workplace do you see picking up lunch or coffee? If you're not someone's assistant, do not get in the habit of acting like one. Sure, maybe there are exceptions when your boss is in fire drill mode or decides to treat a group for getting his coffee—but don't make it a regular thing. And if your male peers aren't chipping in—then you shouldn't be doing it, either.

Don't Be the "Yes" Woman

In the industries I've worked in, there's tremendous pressure to work hard and keep an overflowing plate. Lunch and coffee run aside, it's all too easy to say yes to every project as you strive to "be a good worker bee"—but if you never say no, you'll ultimately just hurt both yourself and your clients. It's essential to stand up for the projects you want to work on, and then push back at other times when you don't have the capacity. You can bet many of the guys say no—and you should, too.

Play to Your Strengths (Even When They're Stereotypes)

Whether it's listening, emotional aptitude, empathy, socializing, or just being the den mother—if you have these strengths, play to them.

They're good qualities to demonstrate as a rising future leader, and, particularly in an environment where those skills are in short supply, they're also not a bad way to get noticed.

Get a Sponsor or join Supporting Organizations

A sponsor is a mentor who will promote you within your industry. And like it or not, it can be nearly impossible to advance as a woman in a male-dominated industry without a sponsor or supporting organization. Start building relationships with other women business leaders—they are going to be your best advocates.

Be Both Confident and Humble

For you to be respected and taken seriously as a young female professional, you need to balance confidence and humility. You will require enough self-confidence to command the respect of your business colleagues, but you need to counter that with humility as there is much that you still don't know. Self-confidence is the highway of commanding, while humility is the highway of getting respect.

Be Open to Learning

For you to grow in your profession, you need to know your limitations and address them. You should always be willing to understand what you don't know by being open to learning. Being agile in your approach will make other people more willing to work with you and take you more seriously. Always assess areas that you need to improve, and humility plays a huge role in convincing your colleagues about your value.

Be Trustworthy

According to research statistics, the majority of people do business with the people that they trust and like. You want to be liked and taken seriously? Being trustworthy provides an automatic default of being taken seriously. Women in business need to establish a trust to their clients for them to be taken seriously.

Nurturing Professional Development

As you help yourself, helping others as a young female professional will earn you respect and develop a view of your leadership skills for others. Try to promote the people around you as you rise in your career. Have some time for offering mentorship, informational interviews, and creating advancement opportunities for others. Being considerate of the growth of colleagues, you will strengthen your relationships with people and contribute to overall company growth.

Respect Others

One of the best ways to earn respect from others is respecting them first. Treat everybody with courtesy from the lowest ranking to the highest ranks. Even though you are advising or critiquing the performance of others, always be appreciative and considerate.

As a female professional in leadership, you can build gradual respect and positive perception from other people by following these guidelines. However, the most important of all is believing in yourself. People get a little mean and critical along the journey. Learn to shake it off and move on.

Who is April Mize-Davis?

April Mize-Davis grew up in a small town called Slapout, Alabama, and was raised on a farm where she learned early in life what hard work is all about, and she knew that farming, as much as she loved it, wasn't going to work for her. April's father, Jimmy Mize, was a successful salesman who worked with John Deere for over 17 years. It was from him she learned her attributes to being successful. She watched her father and the way he built relationships. She learned most importantly that taking the time to listen and treat all your clients as unique individuals would lead to the ultimate success.

She and her sister, Selaine, both went with their dad on many business trips growing up watching their father make things happen. Rarely are the two sisters seen in their home photos without wearing and rocking anything other than a John Deere shirt "Nothing Runs like a Deere." April and her sister are only a year and twelve days apart in age and still to this day the best of friends. April considers herself fortunate to have amazing parents that raised her and her sister both in an incredible, Godly environment and reminded them both daily that God is always watching. Her mother, Delaine, would tell her daily to always cautiously think things through as each day is a new adventure and a gift from God, so don't take things for granted.

Her father's father was Dr. Oliver Samuel Mize and was a nationwide preacher of Christianity and devoted most of his career to prison ministry. He would, in turn, be the minister responsible for getting bibles brought into the prisons throughout the U.S. and started this in Moundsville, West Virginia, which is where her dad grew up. It was from her grandfather that April learned everyone makes mistakes, but it is most important to realize what you learn from them, and never give up on anything.

April also learned a lot from her mother's father, James Chester Bridges. She believes this remarkable man will forever have the most impact on her life and be the one person she admires the most. James was a World War II Corporal in the U.S. Army and received many medals. April considers him the most honest, caring human being she has ever known. It was from him that she learned personal sacrifices would be the hardest ones you ever make and that by giving, you receive blessings that bring happiness back to you. It is because of him she decided to get involved and work with the United States Military, and she realizes that what each military person gives to help keep us protected is something none of us should take for granted. WWII affected her grandfather, and it was something he could never talk about without tears streaming from his face, which inspired her to live life to the fullest. A picture of her Grandfather Bridges and his two brothers (who all fought in WWII at the same time) sits on her desk. April looks at this daily to remind herself that personal sacrifice sometimes comes at a heavy price, and some careers are much harder than others but make the most of them and learn from them.

April realized early on that she had terrific artistic talents as she was always drawing and building things, so it was no surprise that she would put these talents into a career. Growing up a huge Alabama fan, it was evident which college she would attend, i.e., The University of Alabama, where she got a degree in design. As football down in the South is an extremely big deal, April still screams "ROLL TIDE" every fall when her team is playing.

April had some fantastic and influential instructors in college. Still, one stood out more than the others, and that was Dr. Graham in the Engineering Department, who was a registered architect. One day this instructor pulled her aside and said: "April, you are amazingly talented, and you get it and you get architecture and, kid, you are going to go far. I can see the potential in you, and more importantly, you can see it in your eyes. Do you even realize your talents?" This instructor taught architectural design, and he never told the class he was a successful architect just her the day he pulled her aside. April asked him that very day why he never said anything to his students about who he was and had not even acknowledged his architectural accomplishments. His response was something she would always remember, and it sticks with her daily. He said, "April, if I would have told you all who I was and what I have accomplished, then it would have intimidated each of you, and I wanted to be at your level in order to help you all grow and develop." Little did he realize the impact he would have on her career as she too ended up going on to teach college as a design adjunct instructor at Virginia College in Birmingham, Alabama. She taught many classes related to her field of study, but her favorite was Building Construction. She got to make an impact on some amazing students and give back. This was truly one of the best experiences of her career thus far. April will tell you; she loved every minute she was up in a classroom speaking about construction and design.

April has done a lot with her design career. She is an experienced interior designer for both commercial and residential buildings with a lifetime of experience of more than 17 years in this industry. She has worked on more than 500 individual projects and has collaboratively designed on projects that exceeded $1.5 billion in construction cost. She has designed and coordinated with projects that involved the construction of Education Facilities, Churches, Universities, Industrial Complexes, Financial Buildings, Athletic Stadiums, and Healthcare Facilities. Because of her excellent services in the designing industry, she was nominated twice for Cambridge Who's Who among interior designers back in 2007 and 2008.

April has the aspiration that she can influence other women to take chances in a male-dominated industry. She believes that women are as powerful and smart as men, and their voices must be heard. Construction is not just a man's field anymore.

She stated, *"I believe it is an honor to represent Women as an Entrepreneur and leader in my field of Design and Construction, where men are the leaders in this area. It is important that women can be powerful and have an impact, especially in a man dominated field such as construction."*

Furthermore, she said she would like to minimize the obstacles for women, like a young woman not being taken seriously, or how to manage time between family and business in her line of work.

Conversation with April M. Davis *with ADS Design Solutions*

April, can you tell us about you and ADS Designs Solution?

April: I specialize in interior design; however, I have a very diverse background when it comes to the construction world. I started out working in residential design and quickly learned that it was not my passion. I later started doing commercial design and was given the opportunity to work for THE BEST ARCHITECT, in my opinion. He is just an amazing, world-class man of godly integrity, Walter T. McKee of McKee and Associates Architecture and Interior Design in Montgomery, Alabama. It was with his firm that I found my niche.

I specialize in education facilities, athletic facilities, and stadiums. This wonderful man and the folks at this firm taught me everything I know. They will forever be a part of my extended family, from his son, Seawall McKee, who gives me advice daily to everyone else in the company; they are all amazingly talented folks. This firm is like no other as everyone works together and has a healthy respect for each other. I have a strong passion for educational facilities because education is one of those industries that changes frequently and is continually evolving. There is a constant learning curve when it comes to education design. When designing these facilities, I always see new challenges. Aside from doing commercial design, I also specialize in project and construction management and work with clients on overseeing projects from the beginning stages of design to the end result of finished space. I also specialize in Furniture Fixtures and Equipment and spend the majority of my time helping clients with these items and making sure their facilities coincide with the look and design of the space we have created. Design is such a diverse spectrum of so many things, so each client is unique in what I create for them or with them. Some clients might be fully involved in the architecture and design of space, where some choose to let you just do everything and make all the decisions. So, no job is ever the same. This aspect is what makes my job challenging and unique. At the end of the day, I love creating beautiful working environments because "Form MUST Follow Function" as we designers say and live by. So, creating incredible, exquisite, functional spaces is the business I am in, and decking these jobs out from start to finish is my forte.

Tell us about your client base.

April: My client base is anyone who requires design work and wants to create a particular vision from their space to make it uniquely their own, incorporating their own personal touches within these spaces. However, my client base is diverse. I mostly work as a consultant to other architecture firms and contractors who specialize in design-build projects. Some of these clients include McKee Architects, who is always listed as one of the top five architectural firms in Alabama. I have been privileged enough to work with such wonderful contractors as well. Some of these include Steward Construction, where one of my best friends and project managers is Jay Nielson. We have been working together for over 14 years. There's also Rives Construction, who I want to personally point out because this company is just **"hands down one of a kind."** Two of these guys, David Walters and Aaron Wampler, just make construction fun! I am very blessed to have been able to work with them for many years and on many different projects. They always keep me smiling and never ever saw me as just a woman, but as a talented person.

Most importantly, they have always respected me in this field. Other fantastic contractors include Bailey Harris Construction, where Charles Carl and Buddy Bruhn are an absolute pleasure to work with. There's also Beasley Construction Services, Inc., where the owner, Chad Beasley, is a joy to work with, and we have been working together for numerous years. Another great contractor is Thrash Commercial Contractors, Inc., where I recently have gotten to know Jason McCutcheon who hasn't been in the construction field long. However, as a newbie, this young man has so much potential! I can't wait to see what he accomplishes in the future; others include Clements Dean Construction with Justin Dean and Brandon Hartley and Argo Construction, where Joe See was part of Thompson High School construction, and many, many, more but these are a few of my favorites. I specialize in education facilities and have done hundreds of educational facilities across the State of Alabama; this includes K-12th grade schools and higher education facilities such as universities and junior colleges. My biggest accomplishment of design, as well as my favorite and most challenging project, would be the new Thompson High School located in Alabaster, Alabama, where I got to work with one of my favorite School Superintendents, Dr. Wayne Vickers. He and I have been working together for over 14 years doing educational facilities throughout Alabama alongside McKee and Associates Architects. I also have clients in which I design for that require more distinctive unique looks such as Kimber Manufacturing, South Alabama Electric Cooperative, Iberia Bank, and many more.

What I have learned from these larger companies is the branding of their companies is of high importance; adding personal touches that reflect who they are as companies is essential in the design of these spaces. I love getting to know corporations of these sizes and love being able to reflect personal touches in design that represent each one uniquely. I also love working with the U.S. Military. I recently have gotten opportunities to work with Maxwell Air Force Base. Folks such as these are one in a million. They are there to help protect and serve. It is an honor to incorporate designs that reflect such heroic and outstanding individuals who do so much for all Americans.

I also do construction and project management. I enjoy this aspect of the jobs simply because I get to create environments from start to finish and work more on a personal level with folks on these types of projects. I also do FF&E management, and with this, I have had the opportunity to work with many furniture dealers throughout the U.S. I must say it takes a group of folks to help build and produce a completed commercial job. WE ALL must work together to make it happen so that I couldn't do this alone without such companies as Alabama Contract Sales (Clint DeCoux and Rebecca Dowdy), Palmer Hamilton Design (Teri Wilson-Ruggles), Burgess Interiors (Owen Burgess), Hamilton Contract Group (Bain Hamilton), and Virco (John Havicus). These are just a few of my personal favorites that help me make each and every job uniquely special. Some companies have specialized niches like Titan Installations with the owner, Jarrod Parrish, who helps me with all wall covering installs as the sky is the limit when you put the two of us together. We can come up with some craziness to blow folks away. Jarrod is amazingly talented.

Even though I actually do this within my own company, every once in a while, I also get to work alongside some of the best project or program management companies. One that sticks out is Volkert Inc. It is top-notch and a favorite of mine, primarily because of a guy there named Jonathan Grammar, who has taught me so much. He and his family have become close friends of mine. I also couldn't do design without some excellent moving companies. Not many folks realize it, but it takes a village of people to build a village, and commercial jobs are their beast. So having people that can help me do the heavy lifting, such as McCorquodale Transfer with another one of my best friends, Seneca Reid, has been remarkable. He is essential in my business, and I work one-on-one with companies such as these. In my world of design, many different clients and a vast area of my client base are all over the U.S. I love each one of them.

So, having said all of that, I am here to help anyone who wants to create a vision and a distinctive look. I will work with anyone who wants that **ONE OF A KIND** environment to come to full fruition.

Tell me how you differ from your competition.

April: My competition is basically any designer or project management team. The real question is why someone would choose my company or me? I have lots of answers to this question, but the most important reason is I treat each client as a unique entity. I go above and beyond and make all my clients feel special. People ask me all the time what the key to my success is. They want to know how I managed to build a successful business at such a young age. For me to have developed a wide client-base and so quickly, baffles people. Here is my secret. The great Maya Angelou once said, "I've learned that people will forget what you said, people will forget what you did, but people will never forget how you made them feel." This philosophy is the key to success in my business, making people feel amazing. If you do the time, go the extra mile, you will ultimately be successful in anything you set your mind to accomplish. Another key aspect is to have a strong foundation. I was raised in a wonderful Christian environment with loving parents who always conveyed how important God is, and keeping Him first is a huge priority of mine. Matthew 19:26 says, Jesus looked at them and said, "With man this is impossible, but with God all things are possible." The truth of the matter is anyone can build and design a structure, but having the right foundation is the key to building with success and fulfillment. Because without God, nothing is possible. It is important to always give thanks to God and what He has blessed you with; after all, He is the ultimate creator and the one that gave me my special talents of design. So, having a real passion and a positive attitude in this field is what makes me go far in my career endeavors.

I have the mindset of never stopping or letting obstacles stand in the way of my outcomes and visions. This attitude is what makes me stand out as different from others. As part of my success, I surround myself with multitudes of amazing, honest, hardworking people who have the same values as myself. Remember, it takes a village to build such complex commercial facilities, and not all designers can handle complex, multi-story, and high square footage volume projects. Being able to handle pressure, take it in and embrace it, goes a long way in this industry, because it isn't for everyone. Working as a team player is another virtue within this field; it isn't something that can be accomplished by just one individual as they say, "TEAMWORK MAKES THE DREAM WORK." One last and final success factor is always being honest, and if you don't know the answer, be truthful and let it be known. We must remember to be successful; one must always be willing to learn continuously and learn from our mistakes. In my opinion, without mistakes, one isn't learning. We must always strive for perfection in life when doing our passion; without it, we are just mediocre, and no one wants a designer who is only of moderate quality. Design is about making an impression. I want my clients to view me as the one who created a sense of uniqueness for their design. That's what makes me "one of a kind" in this industry.

What constitutes success in your eyes?

April: Success to me is having your clients LOVE you personally and tell you as much. I absolutely LOVE what I do and LOVE my clients. I think of them ALL as my family. I once thought that success meant having material things, and considered these things of the utmost importance. However, I discovered that it is no longer my definition of success. Any successful person can buy materialistic things. The older I have gotten, the more I understand what true success is, and that is being proud of yourself. When you have the support of your family and friends who stand by you, this defines success; especially when you work 24/7 like I do. When my little girl, Madeline, goes with me to see my buildings and says, "Mom, you did good, and this looks amazing, and I love it." Well, let me tell you it doesn't get any better than that. I love the fact that my daughter and my family are proud of me and that seeing my dreams and visions come to life through design happens through a process. The best of success in this world is having the most important folks in your life standing behind you and with you and your clients just saying, "THANK YOU." It is that simple to me. I get true success looking at a completed job saying, "WOW I DID THIS!!!"

Being an entrepreneur isn't easy, and it isn't for everyone. I had to make MANY personal sacrifices building this company and failing at relationships on a personal level is one of them. Sometimes we just get so caught up into building success; we lose sight of the important things in life. Sometimes there just isn't enough time to make for everyone, and that is a judgment call that I believe all of us have to make when building a company. It takes time, dedication, and devotion to build a company. You must put blood, sweat, and tears into it, especially when you are first beginning. Let me say this; there have been a lot of tears in my life along the way. There are days when you just want to walk away and run from it, but what I have realized is the personal sacrifice I have put into my own company is gratification that I just can't imagine not having. It was always my dream to have my own company. It was just a matter of when to take the gamble with myself. I first had to build my name up to where I could be out on my own in this industry. I can say that due diligence is key here. One must do their homework first before they can build a business and be successful at making it, so doing your time first, meaning working for other companies collecting knowledge, is beneficial in establishing your own company. Collect information and talk to others who have successful businesses and figure out the things that were keys to their success and how to avoid making the same mistakes they made. Although sometimes failures are important. We learn a lot from others. These are all keys to a successful business.

Can you share your thoughts on an issue or problem within the design industry?

April: In my industry, we face lots of problems. One being, we take on way too much and get overloaded quickly. Construction never stops. That is the biggest challenge we encounter, and we can't control the weather, which can affect construction progress daily. So, with that, time is always a factor. Sometimes there is just not enough time in the day to get to everyone or every problem we might have. We have to be mindful that questions are always arising in our field of expertise, and we sometimes have to act quickly and make difficult designs on the fly. This is turn means there is NO SUCH THING AS VACATION. I make myself available to my clients 24/7 to handle problems or answer questions. I don't really get a break, but that is the path I choose to take. Sometimes I am a control freak when it comes to my jobs. I want to be able to make the major decisions when it comes to my projects and be completely involved. I eat, sleep, and breathe construction, and I wouldn't have it any other way. When you love what you do, you don't think of it as a job, you think of it as a direct relationship. You just can't get away from it and only choose to stick around for the good parts. Some bad issues must be addressed.

Another problem in this industry is communication skills. We all need to slow down sometimes and take a minute to communicate. Finding clarity helps to resolve issues more directly and deal with things head-on instead of beating around the bush. Sometimes we don't like to admit mistakes and choose to ignore key issues that can result in bigger issues later. We must do a better job of creating a resolution and work together as a team instead of working against each other. I think this is a major problem with a lot of industries; being a team and working as a team is a valuable asset to any good industry.

What are the barriers you are facing in the design business and have you overcome them?

April: I would say the biggest barrier would be being able to balance my work and my personal life. I struggle with this daily. It isn't easy to balance these two things for me. My friends stay on me constantly because they don't see me or even get to talk to me as much. After all, I am constantly working. I am somewhat obsessed with my career and make myself too available to my clients. I also have a hard time saying NO to any new opportunity. I sometimes struggle with taking on too many things at once because I never want to miss out on a new opportunity or what might come from a future endeavor. Finding a balance and taking time for yourself is very important to success because, without it, you can burn yourself out too quickly and start to struggle to make even the simplest decisions. So always take time for yourself and others that are important to you. Remember, jobs can come and go, but your family and friends ultimately are what gives you true happiness, and the joy from these relationships is endless and forever.

Many companies have growth; during the growth, they face Growing Pains! Through the growth of your business, share with us what you feel was your growing pain.

April: One of the biggest obstacles I have faced is being a woman in a man's world. In construction, women aren't well represented, and being taken seriously is a problem, and being respected didn't come easy for me. As a woman, you need to speak your mind and voice your opinion differently because most don't even acknowledge you. I can't tell you how many times I have heard the statement, "that girl oversees this job site," and people just look the other way and not even acknowledge me as a factor in the project. Honestly, sometimes feeling as if my contributions are ignored can be difficult; it is hard not to be respected. In this situation, you must approach things differently. For myself, I acknowledge their attitude and laugh about it. Nothing good comes from conflict, and you will be surprised how folks perceive you once you start working together. They come to realize everyone is equal, and no one is more superior than another human being. We are all different and, ultimately, we all have our niche and what we are good at, and what we can offer to certain jobs to make them successful.

Where do you see yourself in 3 to 5 years in the design industry?

April: Growing, growing, growing, and just getting bigger and better with each day. I would love to hire more individuals and grow my clientele base. I already have some of the most amazing clients, but I want to continue to grow and teach others the key to this business and make a difference. I get a lot of satisfaction in being able to help others as my business grows. I think giving back and being a positive influence on others is important; even helping others in this industry grow is beneficial and impacting. I just plan to continue to keep moving forward with the design community, making lasting friendships, and clients happy with results. Creating spaces and environments with lasting impressions is what I will always strive for; I can't ask for anything more really.

What are you doing to work towards reaching those previously shared goals?

April: I would say I am just trying to work hard and continue to make lasting impressions with my clients and build lifetime relationships with my designs. I just want my clients happy, and I'm working to create amazing spaces and generate repeat business.

As a certified Woman-owned business, why would you recommend to other women in business to become certified?

April: This can open doors that you would have otherwise never imagined possible. There is a limited number of women involved in this organization and being one of the select few is very rewarding and fulfilling. I am honored to be in a group of wonderful and powerful women. By being a part of this organization, you can meet some of the most impactful women, which is an amazing experience. You will meet some pretty incredible individuals. We aren't there to compete with each other but to help one another. I do believe being a part of the women-owned business helps open many avenues. Also, where else can you find a bunch of successful women in one place but in a group like this. The folks involved in this organization are there to help make you more successful and help you achieve any goal you might have. You honestly can't prepare yourself for the friendship and comradery you get from this group

As a woman in a male-dominated industry, what have you done to set yourself apart, i.e., break those barriers?

April: Honestly, just be yourself, and everything else will fall into place. We all have different attributes to give, so gender doesn't matter. We all have something to give in this industry, we all have one common denominator, and that is getting the project up off the ground and getting it finished. Always keep a positive attitude and be respectful. Once respect is gone, nothing will ever get accomplished.

Contact April M. Davis

Email: aprildavisshilland@gmail.com
Business Address: 2024 3rd Ave North Birmingham, AL 35203
LinkedIn Link: https://www.linkedin.com/in/april-davis-shilland-359bb01b/
WB Marketplace: https://brojuremarketplace.com/brojures/943-p-ads-design/pages/0
Phone No: (205) 834-2700

WOMEN IN BUSINESS
LEADING THE WAY

ACKNOWLEDGMENTS

Pamela Stambaugh –

A big thank you to Larry Stambaugh, my husband, for ALL the support you provide me in service of my forever goal to make a difference. I am proud to stand beside you as a partner in our shared and unique missions that make a difference.

To Bill Schwarz, who brought me the Harrison Assessment and Jim Canfield for CEO Tools 2.0.

Special thanks to my clients, who have allowed me the opportunity to contribute to their lives and their businesses as a behavior change catalyst. You make me proud of your successes. Your courage is what makes my contribution possible.

In return, you contribute to my continuing growth and development as a human being and as a professional. You stretch me; you challenge me, you teach me.

Posthumously I wish to acknowledge my parents, William LeRoy and Bethene Anne Larson, for instilling in me the drive, the curiosity, the passion to contribute, to be unstoppable, and who taught me to love my life and the people in it.

And to Landmark Education for the breakthroughs, I continue to experience by being in the inquiry of what it means to be a human being.

I am grateful.

Julie Parmar –

First and foremost, I like to thank Tera with T & S Publishing, LP, for putting this book project together. Many thanks to my amazing co-authors whom I've had the pleasure of getting to know. It was wonderful to collaborate with you all on a business and professional level. Especially, thank you to my family.

Suzanne O'Brien -

To Jax and Blake, you are my "why." To my husband, you are my "how." To my family, thank you for your support. I appreciate everyone who has helped me along my journey and supported me. I am so honored to be apart of this project with such inspiring women!

April Davis –

I would like to thank my sweet daughter Madeline Mize who shares her Mom so much as it isn't easy, my parents Jimmy Mize and Delaine Weldon for always supporting me in my career. My sister Selaine and her husband, Tim Hayes, who help me raise my little girl. Special thanks to my wonderful Uncle, Jeff Mize, who always listens and gives me fantastic advice, and his son, Cody Mize, who works for me at times and puts up with me. Thanks to Walter and Seawell McKee of McKee and Associates, who gave me my start in commercial architecture. To fellow co-workers who have done nothing but support my career, I thank you. Many times you have helped me through the hard personal times. Thanks to Neil Hughes and his beloved sister, Amanda Hughes-Beckwith, (my best friend and my right hand; may you rest in peace as I miss you every day). Thanks to Bobby Dennis, Lisa Bowen, and Jay Evans. Lastly, to some fantastic colleagues who have impacted me in so many ways, Rebecca Dowdy and Clint DeCoux (ACS), Seneca Reed (McCorquodale Transfer), David Walters, and Aaron Wampler (Rives Construction), and Starr Berthelot (Iberia Bank). I LOVE YOU ALL !!!!

Kristen Billingsley –

Thank you for this opportunity to work with these amazing ladies and share my story. I am grateful for everything and everyone that have assisted me on my journey, from my kids, family, old friends, new friends, employees, strangers, human angels, angels, and every experience. May my heart and soul continue to build commUNITY and grow with love and light as we journey together.

Leticia Latino van-Splunteren –

To my parents, Baldassare and Giuseppa Latino, the best mentors I could have had. Dad, you showed me that it's not a matter of IF, it is a matter of HOW. Problems will never cease to be there; our reaction to them is what sets us apart. You have always supported me and my decisions, even knowing sometimes ahead of time that I was going to get burned. You let things play out so that I could build my own experience.

Mom, your commitment to our family and your generous heart inspire me every day. You once told me that you didn't want a professional career because you thought there was no more important job than raising self-confident, accomplished, and kind human beings.

You embody the definition of a successful woman without having had a business career!

To my husband, Don, because in our adventure together, we materialized the most significant gifts in anyone's life, our children.

To Christian and Emma, you inspire me to be better every day!

Special Thanks to my dear friend and 'Editor-in-Chief,' Enrica, who is always there ready with honest advice to make my writing so much better!

Love and gratitude to all.

Lauren Sustek –

This is dedicated to my Father, who taught me to think big, dream on, and get back up when I fall; to my Mother who always stressed the importance of having family in my life; and to the fantastic people that make up my team...you know who you are. I can't imagine this life without you. Forever grateful to you all.

Marci Klein –

Special thanks to:

My two boys, Blake and Tyler, for wanting their own room. Without their encouragement, I would still be working in my home office instead of my own production studio.

My husband, Ken, for encouraging me to go back into the video business after staying home as Mom for so many years.

The Pink Shoe Sisters for taking this journey with me. You all inspire me with your personal stories of success, your compassion, and for just being you.

Tera at T & S Publishing for asking me to be a part of this collaborative book. I had always dreamed of being an author, and Tera made my dream into a reality.

To all my past clients, for believing in me and trusting me with your video stories. To my future clients who I have not had the pleasure to work with yet.

To Brian, my amazing assistant, I'm gonna' miss you when you move on.

To all my associates in broadcast television. We laughed, we cried, we argued, we worked crazy hours, you edited me, I edited you... but in the end, I learned so much from you. Thanks for sharing the industry with me.

To Ed, Brian, and Miles... for meeting me in the surf line-up every week.

Patty Taulbee –

I am extremely grateful for all the people that have been part of my life's journey (you know who you are). Through the valleys and hilltops, I would not be me without you!

Bonni Shevin-Sandy -

I am a proud WBENC for over a decade!. I've made unbelievable friends and amazing new clients. I want to personally thank Emilia DiMenco, Karen Goldner, my WBENC champions!

During publishing my first book, I lost both my parents within 18 months, I am the only living child, I wouldn't have had the strength or the perseverance without my family, and friends. Lisa Esz, Dylan Esz, Matthew Esz.. Mindy and Neal Kaplan and family, Debbie and Auggie Garcia and family, My partner at Diversitypromos.com, Dorothy Adams, and family. Besides these incredible best friends, I am forever grateful to have the support from my amazing husband of almost 30 years, Jeffrey Sandy.

Last but certainly never the least, my three amazing sons, who I'm proud to have raised three remarkable young men. As I tell them, people aren't going to remember everything you bought them, but, hopefully, they will remember everything you taught them! My sons are fantastic people and my best friends! I am truly blessed! My parents guided me, but this particular aunt, more like a mother, Elinor Grant, helped guide me from my childhood forward. MY patient best friends, "The Couples club - My parents best friends, Ben and Heidi Rosenberg, and the "Couples Club" I LOVE YOU ALL!

Amy Reisinger –

There are many people I must thank for having the energy and ability to complete this chapter. To my family and friends, I cherish you all. Thank you for all your love and support. And mostly for having faith in me through this rollercoaster of a ride.

To my husband, Eric, and son, Joe: I am so thankful that I have you both in my corner pushing me when I am ready to give up. Thanks for not just believing in me, but knowing that I could do this! I Love You Always & Forever!

To TeamFusion: Thank God for all of you! For being my support system, sounding board, and staying by my side through thick and thin for all these years. Especially to Autumn Miller:

One of the most ethical and loyal women I have ever met. Thank you for all you do and continue to do.

I am grateful to my mentors who have shaped my life and helped me learn these truths.
And finally, to God be the glory for all the many blessings I have received in this ridiculous, incredible adventure.

Marianne Ellis –

Thank you to the CEO at WBENC Summit & Salute, who was crying after a failed MatchMaker Meeting and trusted me. If I hadn't impromptu coached her to success, my career, company, and this book chapter would not exist.

To Summer Sepulveda for pushing me into coaching and speaking, Pamela Williamson for trusting me with her signature WBEC-West Platinum Supplier Program and Joycelyn Yue for hiring me as an SCE EDGE Business Coach. To Russel Wohlwerth for showing me the procurement ropes and Renee Hill Young for introducing me to WBENC.

To my Co-Founder Janet Lienhard for helping make CEO Success Community a reality and Sue Berg for joining us. To the CEOs of CEO Success Community, thank you for letting me share your inspiring stories.

Finally, to Tera Jenkins, Debra Englander, my husband David, my mom Gloria, Lauren & Mark thanks for your support. And, to my Pink Shoe Book Sisters — "We did it!"

Joan Brothers –

Bruce - My Father, for always being supportive

Bev - My Aunt, for always being at the ready and a special thanks for the handholding.

Bill - My husband, for being so encouraging and showing me many opportunities.

William - My son, for always keeping me on my toes.

From the Publisher -

A Special Thank You for your support goes out to-

Two Chics in the City Podcast - hosts Tracy Swain and JaVonne Williams for the extremely informative interviews and featuring the authors on your podcast.

Check them out at www.twochicsinthecity.com

The Lighter Soul Podcast – host Angela Moore – for insightful and delightful podcast interviews of the Pink Shoe Sisters!

Catch an episode at www.alightersoul.com